STILL Blaming Children

Youth Conduct and the Politics of Child Hating

by Bernard Schissel

Fernwood Publishing • Halifax

Dedication

to Wendy, Nathan and Matthew

Editing: Douglas Beall and Brenda Conroy
Cover painting: "Cross My Heart, Hope to Die" by Marie Lannoo
Photo of cover painting: AK Photos, Saskatoon
Printed and bound in Canada by: Hignell Book Printing Limited

Fernwood Publishing is grateful for the permission granted to reprint photos and copy-
right material used in this publication.

Published in Canada by Fernwood Publishing
Site 2A, Box 5, 32 Oceanvista Lane
Black Point, Nova Scotia, B0J 1B0
and 324 Clare Avenue, Winnipeg, Manitoba, R3L 1S3
www.fernwoodbooks.ca

Fernwood Publishing Company Limited gratefully acknowledges the financial support
of the Department of Canadian Heritage and the Canada Council for the Arts for our
publishing program

NOVA SCOTIA Tourism and Culture

Canadian Heritage   Patrimoine canadien

The Canada Council for the Arts
Le Conseil des Arts du Canada

Library and Archives Canada Cataloguing in Publication

Schissel, Bernard, 1950-
Still blaming children : youth conduct and the politics of child hating /
Bernard Schissel.

ISBN 10: 1-55266-186-5 ISBN 13: 978-1-55266-186-4

1. Juvenile delinquency--Canada. 2. Juvenile delinquency--Canada--Public
opinion. 3. Juvenile justice, Administration of--Canada. 4. Canada--Legal
status, laws, etc.--Canada. I. Title.

HV9108.S342 2006   364.36'0971   C2006-900214-2

Contents

Acknowledgements

I am indebted to many people for their encouragement and assistance with this book. First, I wish to express my gratitude to my colleagues in the Department of Sociology at the University of Saskatchewan for their support, and to the University of Saskatchewan Office of Research Services Publication Fund. I am indebted, as well, to the Social Sciences and Humanities Research Council of Canada (grant number 41-095-1532). I would like to thank my research associates, Lauren Eisler and Trina Evitts, for their competence and dedication. Many thanks to Carolyn Brooks for her interest in this work and her generous input.

I would also like to express my gratitude to Errol Sharpe and the staff of Fernwood Publishing for their support and their commitment to relevant scholarly work. As always, it has been a pleasure working with Wayne Antony on this project, and I am grateful to him for his insights, expertise and academic vitality. Thanks also to Brenda Conroy for copy editing, Bev Rach for designing the cover and the book, and Debbie Mathers for typing the final changes to the manuscript.

Lastly, I would like to thank my sons Nathan and Matthew for their youthful spirit and for making me laugh and, most importantly, Wendy, whose unwavering support, editorial ability and intellect have made this project a joy.

Foreword

In 1997, I completed *Blaming Children: Youth Crime, Moral Panics and the Politics of Hate.* I knew that the world was becoming a rather unpleasant place for children and youth and that media constructions of dangerous, deviant youth were part of the reason. The media stories were blatant in their racist, sexist, classist and ageist rhetoric. The depictions were often of young people who were identified and stereotyped by their socio-economic and demographic characteristics and who were condemned largely because of their phenotypical characteristics. The language that framed their deviance was vile and in many ways stood outside the boundaries of human rights protections, specifically the right to be safe from acts of hate. Some of this original hate literature is reproduced and discussed Chapters 4 and 5. The condemnatory rhetoric in news reports often echoed popular discourse. In fact, the new *Youth Criminal Justice Act* was being developed at that time and the framework and mantra for the Act was "public safety." Politicians and policy makers were intent on appeasing conservative voters, who were caught up in the torrent of fear of kids, partly the result of some highly sensationalized crimes by a very few young people. The new youth justice bill had two rather contradictory tenets: societal protection in the form of harsh justice for dangerous youth, and child and youth welfare in the form of extra-judicial provisions to keep kids out of the justice system. An interesting combination of the two policy sentiments occurred in the sentencing provisions of the Act, which were constructed, in theory, to address the reality that Canada locks up more young people than any other jurisdiction in the industrialized world and that youth receive harsher sentences in Canada than do adults. Interestingly, the sentencing provisions of the Act only went as far as ensuring that children and youth, in some instances, could be sentenced as adults. I expected, and in progressive societies one should be able to expect, that children and youth would get special considerations and that concessions in sentencing would go well beyond those for adults. The Act does contain rhetoric to this effect in terms of extra-judicial measures and special considerations for age, gender and race, but the guidelines are clear that young people should be sentenced "equally" with adults.

Until I decided to embark on a sequel to *Blaming Children,* I assumed that at least the rhetoric surrounding young offenders — and youth in general — had become more benign and enlightened since the late 1990s. As I began to write *Still Blaming Children,* I came to the realization that nothing much had changed. While, the actual journalistic language is the same, claims to objectivity have become more forceful. The new journalism of youth crime invokes science and research more than in the past, although the role of experts has always been important in "political journalism." The current journalism of youth is still fraught with stereotypes of race, class, gender and age, but it is also infused with a contemporary discourse of health that has a decidedly socio-biological bias, incorporating issues of unhealthy maternity, birth defects, learning disabilities, poor child-rearing and culture. The "science" of medicine now seems to frame discussions of young people and immorality with a condemnatory language of socio-cultural stereotyping.

As I said in *Blaming Children*

> the attack on children has become good business and good politics. Almost without exception, election platforms from parties of all political philosophies contain promises to get tough on kids. It is as if children have become the new enemy of the state. They are easy to attack because they are disenfranchised and because they have very few avenues of redress. They are, in essence, the perfect scapegoats.

At the time of writing of this sequel, the Canadian electorate has voted in a Conservative minority government — a party combined from the old Reform and Progressive Conservative parties — which campaigned, in part, on a "get tough on youth crime" platform. Ironically and distressingly, the other three major parties, all politically left of the Conservative Party, campaigned on similar justice platforms. In part, the campaigns were part of the aftershock of the 2005 Boxing Day shooting of a young girl in a Toronto shopping mall by a supposed "gang member." While the crime was heart-breaking and pointless, the political fallout was predictable. All parties called for a war on crime, especially on young people's crime.

As this book reveals, very little has changed since 1997. In fact, the inflammatory rhetoric may be more severe as it is infused with the rhetoric of science including the medical and forensic detection of risk. This is, as I discuss in Chapter 7, partly the result of the global position of children and youth. Essentially, I argue that the condemnation of children and youth in popular cultural discourse is closely tied to the reality that youth are, now more than ever, exploited for their labour, their consumption and their sexuality. Justifying the immorality of children and youth through public discourse and public policy is the first, and an essential, step in the exploitation of a largely disenfranchised young population.

CHAPTER 1

Crime, Justice, and the Condemnation and Exploitation of the Young

A crescendo of anxious voices lamented the proliferation of the poor and unproductive in the towns and villages of England. Moralists constantly complained about the swarms of idle and dissipated young people who were not being contained within the system of household discipline — the system on which, most people believed, social stability depended. Stability in the state, Tudor preachers never tired of reminding their congregations, rested on stability in the family. (Underdown 1992: 11–12)

The Development of Youth Justice and the Erosion of Child Protection

Whether Canadians like to admit it or not, Canada's war on crime, like the war on crime in many other countries, and in other eras (as described above), has, in an important sense, become a war against youth. With proposals to reintroduce the death penalty for young killers or implement mandatory boot camps for all young offenders, Canadian society is embarking on a crusade to increase punishment for children, ostensibly, in the hopes of curbing crime.

The focal point for this law-amd-order campaign was the *Young Offenders Act* (1982), which was replaced by the *Youth Criminal Justice Act* (2003). The *Young Offenders Act* was struck to give youth the same rights and freedoms as their adult counterparts. It replaced the *Juvenile Delinquents Act* (jda) of 1908, which was based on the principle of *parens patriae*, that the state is the ultimate guardian of the child. The jda gave the state the right to override the civil liberties of the child and the family and to intervene forcibly in family life. This welfare approach to childhood essentially gave juvenile authorities wide discretionary powers in the informal policing of juveniles.

In response, the *Young Offenders Act* (yoa) was ordained to re-establish the legal rights of youth. The Act was intended to ensure several things: that accused youth would be adequately represented in court; that their parents or guardians would be informed of their arrest and would be directed to appear in court; that accused youth would be informed of their rights and every effort made to ensure that they are able to make informed decisions about their legal options; and that the names and other references of the accused would be kept in confidence, safe from public scrutiny. Most importantly, however, the yoa was supposed to ensure that young offenders, whenever possible, would be directed away from the formal legal process and toward alternative measures, including community-based programs of reparation and mediation. So, in the final analysis, the principles of the yoa were declared, in general, to protect the civil liberties of young people and specifically, to provide them with non-judicial options.

The 1984 implementation of the *Young Offenders Act*, however, did not ameliorate the concerns of critics, who argued that the youth justice system continued to avoid the issue of what they perceived to be an increase in crime rates for Canadian youth. They argued that it was too lenient, that youth were not deterred because of the soft punishments allotted under the Act, and that it allowed for the release of dangerous adolescent offenders into society. The harshest critics, usually found within groups that followed a "law-amd-order" ideology, such as police organizations and victim's rights groups, argued that the Act lacked punitive measures and placed undue emphasis on the rights of the offender while ignoring the rights of the victims of crime. Ex-police officer turned author Carsten Stroud (1993), in his book *Contempt of Court: The Betrayal of Justice in Canada,* underscores the position taken by these critics with his claim that police cynically refer to the *Young Offenders Act* as the Youth Protection Act. Less punitive-minded critics believed that the problems with the Act had roots, not so much in the legislation itself, but in its administration. They charged the provinces with failing to implement some of the Act's more treatment-oriented provisions. Provincial administrators countered by arguing that the yoa was a complicated piece of legislation and difficult to make work (Tanner 1996).

Numerous amendments were proposed to deal with the criticisms aimed at both administration and content of the yoa (Bell 2002). Bill C-106 was introduced in the House of Commons on April 30, 1986, and passed by the Senate on June 26, 1986. This first amendment to the Young Offenders Act focused mainly on technical and procedural aspects of the law (Winterdyk 2000). A further amendment, Bill C-12, which came into force in of 1992, increased maximum sentences for murder from three to five years, outlined continuation of custody provisions and clarified rules for transferring youth to adult court (Winterdyk 2000: 447).

Bill C-37, put forward in 1994 and declared in force on the first of December 1995, represented another attempt by the federal government to balance the demands of competing groups for changes to the *Young Offenders Act*. It increased the maximum sentences for murder to ten years, created a presumption of transfer to adult court for sixteen to seventeen year olds charged with serious offences and allowed written victim impact statements in youth court. In total, there were nine relatively punitive recommendations put forward by Bill C-37, which formed the basis for Bill C-68.

The *Youth Criminal Justice Act*

Bill C-68, introduced in the House of Commons on March 11, 1999, came into force as the *Youth Criminal Justice Act* in April 2003. The new Act attempts to address concerns put forward from both those who argue for more punitive actions and those who argue for the need for special considerations for youth who come into conflict with the law. Public safety and security are now at the core of youth justice. To ensure public safety, the new Act includes the possibility for strong punitive measures to be employed against youth who are considered dangerous, violent or habitual offenders. Ontario's Ministry of the Attorney General made over a hundred recommendations to the federal government on ways to make young offenders more accountable for violent acts, including to automatically try and sentence sixteen and seventeen year olds as adults when they are charged with a serious, presumptive offence such as murder, attempted murder or manslaughter (Ministry of the Attorney General 2000). According to Justice Canada the primary features of the new *Youth Criminal Justice Act* address the following issues: strong community sentencing measures for youth in conflict with the law; diversion by both police and prosecution; and new, intensive rehabilitation custody and supervision sentences, including custody in adult prisons, available for offenders convicted of presumptive offences. According to section 2 of the *Youth Criminal Justice Act*, presumptive offences are offences committed by a young offender over the age of fourteen and include first and second degree murder, manslaughter, aggravated sexual assault and violent offences equivalent to those for which an adult would be liable to imprisonment for more than two years. The new sentences also apply to youth with mental illnesses, psychological disorders and emotional disturbances, thus allowing youth justice court judges to direct treatment and programming but also to deal with offenders designated as dangers to public safety.

The new Act incorporates several other features: 1) the option for youth with patterns of repeat offending to receive adult sentences at the age of fourteen years and older; 2) the publication of names of youth convicted of a crime who receive adult sentences; 3) the provision for a sentence of up to two years in jail for a parent who willfully fails to supervise his or her children when the parent has an undertaking with the court (Department of Justice Canada 1999 .

The Repercussions of a More Punitive Form of Youth Justice

Youth justice reform in Canada, over several years culminating in the *Youth Criminal Justice Act*, has served to erode the protection/welfare philosophy towards children and youth and has replaced it with a societal safety, just-desserts agenda (Hogeveen and Smandych 2001). The historical development of a Canadian youth criminal justice system appears to represent a transfer from the notion that children were essentially "adults in training," to a belief that children were in need of protection and welfare, to an attempt to balance the needs of youth with the rights of society in regard to public safety. It is arguable that recent youth crime legislation reflects an increasingly tough attitude that youth should be held accountable for their deeds and that parents should be punished for the delinquent or criminal actions of their offspring. As a result, "the focus of policies to curb youth crime seems to be increasingly on families and individuals rather than society as a whole (Alvi 2000: 38). Further, Giroux (2003a) has alerted us to the reality that the politics of individualization — the notion that crime lives within individuals — is accompanied by state policy that valorizes and privileges "privatization, deregulation, consumption, and safety" (xix). It is interesting in this context that increasingly punitive youth justice laws accompany increasing corporate sovereignty and increasing campaigns by corporations to target youth as the new super-consumers.

The generalized law-amd-order mindset in Canada, and many other countries, that is typified by the *Youth Criminal Justice Act*, especially the provisions that are intended to protect the public, seems to stand in contradistinction to the overall principles of earlier incarnations of youth justice in Canada. Those early provisions held that prevention and rehabilitation were constructive, that young people needed their judicial rights protected and that punishment and public condemnation were ultimately destructive to the young offender and to society. Interestingly, the *Young Offenders Act* and the *Youth Criminal Justice Act*, in their original conceptions, were both based on progressive, compassionate provisions that embodied like intentions: 1) to foster the use of community-based, non-carceral alternatives to formal punishment; 2) to provide short-term maximum sentences for even the most dangerous offenders; 3) to minimize labelling through the insurance of anonymity through publication bans; 4) to provide civil rights of the young offender through adequate legal and parental representation in court.

Fiscal and political realities have dictated that the progressive provisions of Canadian youth justice have become supplanted by orthodox law-amd-order policies, which are driven by lack of funding and an obsession with public protection. The changes brought about by the new law insure that "soft," non-serious offenders are cut adrift because of lack of alternatives and more serious offenders are dealt with in a more draconian fashion than before, through longer sentences and transfers to adult facilities. Programs and organization systems that were supposed to replace the formal justice system under the ycja have been poorly realized, and police and court officials have been left with little alternative but to use the formal legal code in ministering to young offenders, especially repeat and serious offenders. The state's inability to support the spirit and intent of the alternative measures provision of the ycja has given right-wing political movements ample fodder for their "we told you so" agenda. With the rise in the number of "street kids" (which is certainly a social/political problem and not a criminological phenomenon) and with a profusion of highly publicized violent crimes committed by youth, the "war on young offenders" is a *cause celebre* that politicians seem unable to resist. And, as we will come to see, the discourse of "gangs" permeates the contemporary public consciousness.

Still Blaming Children

If we were in the beginning stages of a "moral panic" that indicted children and adolescents, especially the marginalized and disadvantaged, for their dangerousness and their growing disrespect of adults (as I argued in *Blaming Children*), I contend that the *fin de siecle* moral panic has grown into a much more subtle and powerful social movement against kids. The end result of the condemnation of young people is the continuing scapegoating of youth for political purposes, and, in keeping with the irony of punishment, the alienation of a more uncompromising, more disaffiliated youth population. Increasing punishment, while denying access to civic and political involvement, greatly increases the likelihood of alienation and ultimately of young people's antisocial behaviour. Despite the political rhetoric to the contrary, we do not collectively consider children our most valuable resource. In fact, we consider them one of our most dangerous threats.

Our collective disintegrating wish to protect children in our society is the focus of this book. I explain the nature and the extent of the moral panic about youth criminogenesis by discussing the role of the media and its affiliations with information/political systems, with its readers/viewers and with corporate Canada. The current political pastime of "blaming children" for all social evils is placed in the context of changing international, national and local agendas. I contend that public panics are predictable in that they have little to do with a criminogenic reality, but much to do with the economic and political context in which they arise. Furthermore, crime panics are targeted at vulnerable and marginal people. In fact, a critical analysis of media coverage brings us to a particular political moral position: the public perception of seriousness of crime is largely a matter of misjudgements and fear about race, geography and family constitution. I argue further that the panic that vilifies children is a coordinated, calculated attempt to nourish the ideology that supports a society stratified on the bases of race, class and gender and that the war on kids is part of the state-business mechanism that continually reproduces an oppressive social and economic order through both labour and consumer exploitation (Giroux 2003a; Hall, et al 1978, Iyengar and Kinde 1987, Herman and Chomsky 1988).

Ironically, this country is prepared to ignore the reality that:

- there is little real increase in serious youth crime;
- that participation rates in criminal activities are relatively stable;
- that youth crime is comprised mostly of petty, unthinking acts;
- that the increase in official rates of youth criminal behaviour is largely the result of increased arrest rates;
- the courts have adopted a zero-tolerance mentality;
- that society is largely unable to provide effective alternatives to punishment; and
- that, most importantly, the things for which youth are arrested and incarcerated are matters of health much more than they are matters of criminality, drug abuse being the most obvious example.

I do not mean to imply that there are no habitual young offenders, some of whom are dangerous. However, not only does the general public perceive that youth crime is on the rise, but conventional analysts, including some progressive, critical ones defend the political move to a more punitive youth crime policy on the basis of a more dangerous, criminogenic youth population. Despite the analytical polemics, most Canadian cities are confronted by high-risk youth, many of whom are "on the street" and vulnerable to exploitation by adults. Such youth often retaliate aggressively. Habitual and potentially dangerous offenders are a small minority, but only their activities seem to inform the moral panic debates. And of course, their own victimization and disadvantage disappear in the accounts of their dangerousness.

As political movements come to terms with their "terror of adolescents," the debates seem to coalesce around the suffering of those who are victims of violent crime. The fear of crime, which seems to be forever increasing, is a powerfully personal and politically emotional tool. Ironically, the fear of kids in Canada has been fuelled by two phenomena that are largely the result of business as usual.

First, part of the problem has been the increased visibility of young people in public places. As industry "rationalizes" production by reducing

employment costs, youth unemployment rises, to as high as 30 percent in some regions. Simply put, more youth have increasingly more idle time, and the work that is available is poorly paid, bereft of benefits and offers little in terms of meaningful apprenticeship. The typical employee at a fast food outlet is an adolescent, the typical wage is at or just above minimum wage, the work is typically hard and quite dangerous, and the typical benefits package is non-existent. Furthermore, centralized shopping centres built with profits rather than community solidarity in mind, have become gathering placed for unemployed adolescents. While their presence is not discouraged by private interests, large numbers of youth in places such as shopping malls fuel the panic that kids are loitering with intent. As I argue in the following chapter, the reality for children and youth in a global world is labour exploitation and consumer "abuse." The irony is that youth are badly needed in bourgeoning capitalism, but they are condemned either through omission or by commission.

Second, most people gain their images and opinions about the nature and extent of crime through the media. In Canada, much of our vicarious experience with youth crime is filtered through Canadian and American television. American news, much of which teeters on the brink of fiction, is highly sensational, selective to time and place, and focuses primarily on dangerous individuals. I argue that such depictions are not based on reality but rather on the wants of a presumed audience. The news industry argues that their function is to present news accounts that are based on an objective reality. More likely, however, the industry constructs the news to appeal to the demands of a frightened audience and a political-economic system that casts blame. Especially in a post–9/11 era, news is more controlled than in the past and the freedom of speech that journalists traditionally depended upon to be good journalists is much more tenuous (Chomsky 2002).

What we are left with is a gulf between reality and perception. The reality is that youth are mostly disenfranchised from the democratic process at all levels of governance, they are disadvantaged in the labour market and they have few services available to them, unlike their adult counterparts. When they do break the law, they are most likely to victimize other disadvantaged youth. Although youth crime has not increased significantly in recent years, the prosecution of youth crime has. That reality stands in stark contrast to the singular collective perception that kids are out of control, that they are more dangerous now than ever and that youth crime is expanding at an alarming rate. How do we explain the existence of a belief system that moralizes about and condemns children in the face of contradictory evidence? Are we, as a society, so uncertain about our ability to raise children that we constantly question the culture of youth? Are we, in an adult-created and based world, so unfamiliar with adolescent social conventions that we are frightened by the unfamiliar? Or, are there structural forces at work that construct, communicate and perpetuate a belief system that benefits those who have access to power and indicts those who live on the margins of society? Fear is a great motivator. Society's growing fear of kids, its moral panic about their criminogenesis, has significant power to marginalize and disenfranchise young people.

Moral Panics and Power

One of the important considerations in understanding moral panics as historical and socio-political phenomena is that they are not unique and evolutionary, but that they occur regularly and predictably throughout history. Much of the moral panic literature, common in critical criminological research of the late sixties and early seventies, used historical analyses to study the phenomenon of putative crime waves and the origins of public panics about crime (Hall et al. 1978; Cohen 1980). The research concentrated on how atypical or rare events at particular historical junctures came to raise the collective ire to the point where the public demanded law reform. In addition, the literature concentrated on how official and popular culture accounts of criminality were based on over-generalized, inaccurate and stereotypical descriptions of criminals and their associations, and how the public panics that resulted were mostly directed at working class or marginalized people. Much of the research, in addition, concentrated on moral panics over youth crime, especially in relation to alienated, organized, gang-based delinquents.

Stanley Cohen's (1980) influential work developed the concept of moral panic to study and make sense of British society's alarm and attack on youth in the 1960s and early 1970s. His analysis of the construction of the "Mods and Rockers" illustrated how this political/linguistic device, based on social stereotyping, came to circumscribe youth misconduct. He also illustrated how the media, through their abilities to use evocative language and imagery, alerted the public to a potentially criminogenic youth, coined by Cohen as "folk devils." Cohen discovered that once the folk devil was identified by the mainstream media, the context for understanding youth crime was established. For example, the judiciary and the police overreacted to those identified as gang members and came to view the Mods and Rockers as a conspiratorial, well-organized force. The media as well were inordinately preoccupied with understanding the youth malefactor as a gang member and dangerous youth as organized conspiracies of defiance.

Equally important as the critical analysis of the media and political motives, however, was Cohen's specification of the connection between the particular moral panic he described and the social, political and economic atmosphere of 1960s England:

> The sixties began the confirmation of a new era in adult-youth relations.... What everyone had grimly prophesied had come true: high wages, the emergence of a commercial youth culture 'pandering' to young people's needs... the permissive society, the coddling by the Welfare State.... The Mods and Rockers symbolized something far more important than what they actually did. They touched the delicate and ambivalent nerves through which post-war social change in Britain was experienced. No one wanted depression or austerity.... Resentment and jealousy were easily directed at the young because of their increased spending power and sexual freedom. (1980: 192)

Hall et al. (1978) lent a more Marxist interpretation to the historical understanding of moral panics by suggesting that panics serve a decidedly elitist purpose. Their study of mugging in England in the 1970s suggested that the public and political alarm over street crime was created by the ruling elite to divert attention away from the crisis in British capitalism. As in other capitalist countries, increasing unemployment was being deliberately used by business and government to re-establish general profit levels and fight inflation. In essence, high profits and high employment are anathema and inflationary. The British industrial state was in fiscal and social distress. To deflect attention away from the real causes of the fiscal crisis, according to Hall et al. (1978), authorities exaggerated the threat posed by street crime.

The work of Hall and his co-authors is particularly instructive in that it studies the connections between ideological production, the mass media and those in positions of power. Without this type of critical perspective, we are left with the presumption that the media act alone, isolated from economy and politics, and that their mistaken mandate is the result of poor journalism and the requirement to compete in the supply and demand world of news. Just as I argue in this book, Hall et al. contend that one of the primary functions of the news is to give political significance to events. In fact, the media both draw on and re-create consensus. This contention becomes apparent when we realize that the "media represent the primary, and often the only source of information about many important events and topics" (1978: 56). Furthermore, "the media define for the majority of the population what significant events are taking place, but, also, they offer powerful interpretations of how to understand these events" (1978: 57).

(For more current debates, see Roberts and Foehr 2004; Fleras and Kunz 2001.) One of the important ways in which the news media maintain their power is by claiming journalistic objectivity as *a priori*. The ostensible task of news media is to sift fact from fiction, and they do this by drawing on expert opinion. As we will come to see later in this book, expert opinion is an extremely common journalistic device and such opinion is generally as wide and varied as it is numerous.

The discourse of news media is, first and foremost, ideological, that is, the language is morality-laden and belongs to privileged, powerful people. There is a structured relationship between the media and the ideas of the powerful sectors of the society. The creation, control and proliferation of journalistic discourse is constrained by definitions of right and wrong that are governed by powerful people, even if such people do not hold with such definitions. Capitalist power is able reproduce a morality that implies that certain people are better and more valuable than others on the basis of their place in the economic system. Such discourse serves to reproduce the relations of production (the socio-economic system that allows some to live in mansions while requiring others to live on the streets) by organizing the way we think of crime and punishment in relation to poverty and wealth. Crime, as it is constructed and framed in public discourse, functions to legitimate and maintain class differences in all sectors of the society. I show later on in this book, as well, that rarely do media accounts that equate crime with privation do so without discussing related issues of visible minority group membership (and immigration) along with the problems that single motherhood poses to traditional family values.

Many of the panics that typified the sixties and seventies appear today in similar form, if not content. In moral panics, public perceptions of the degree and form of violent crime are largely inaccurate and exaggerated (Kappeler, Blumberg and Potter 1993; Painter 1993; Jenkins 1992). While traditional research on moral panics dealt with "mainstream" deviances — drug use, witchcraft, for example — current research tends to concentrate on what might be labelled shocking or lurid deviances: ritual abuse, serial killers, paedophilia and child abuse. While not to diminish the seriousness of these crimes, it is important to note that, with the exception of child abuse, most of these phenomena are quite rare. And as typified by past moral panics, the rare occurrences nourish a general alarm over individual safety.

There is, on the other hand, a rapidly expanding body of literature that focuses on youth gangs, studying either the origins and activities of such gangs or the public reactions to them. This rather orthodox, narrow-focused literature tends to endorse public panic discourse and, distressingly,

discourse about the racialized nature of crime. By ignoring the moral out-
rage that greets all youth, not just identifiable gang members, it uses race
and gang membership to underscore the presumed violent and organized
nature of youth crime. This is not to suggest that the moral panic surrounding youth crime is subtle or hidden. On the contrary, the attack on youth
has been vocal, concerted and politicized, fostered by the portrayal of id-
iosyncratic examples of youth crime as typical. The existing public debates
on youth crime, while largely uninformed, have the potency and the scientific legitimacy to direct public opinion and to effect social control policy
that stigmatizes and controls those who are most disadvantaged and most
victimized.

The primary effect of media and official accounts of youth crime is to
decontextualize such acts for public consumption. Although the media may
not directly control public opinion, they are certainly able to contain the nature of discourse by establishing parameters of discussion and by giving the
appearance of consensus on public issues. The portraits of youth criminals
that public crime accountants paint are largely of nihilistic, pathological
criminals who act alone or as members of gangs, criminals who are devoid
of a moral base. The decontextualization of youth crime, however, misses a
fundamental consideration in understanding crime: most repeat young offenders and their families are victims of socio-economic conditions beyond
their control, and they are more than likely to be repeatedly victimized as
clients of the systems of law, social welfare and education.

The powerful benefit from a particular "truth" about young offenders.
Media images push public discussions away from understandings of youth
crime that include the effects of privation, disenfranchisement and marginalization, and toward misunderstanding youth crime as individual immorality and pathology. Those in power in a corporate or state context are largely
responsible for creating conditions that are detrimental to those without
power. The attack on government deficits and the unrelenting drive to cut
taxes, which seem currently to drive considerable public policy initiatives,
are detrimental to the least advantaged but advantageous to the already
privileged. For example, state policy rarely attacks unfair or non-progressive
taxation, ostensibly for fear of alienating business and driving it elsewhere,
especially in the context of free trade zones, like nafta. The recourse then
is to attack social support programs, employment initiatives and education.
The system of profit is absolved from responsibility for making the lives
of the disenfranchised poor more precarious, for destroying social support
networks. The law, in its function as moral arbiter, has a significant input
into the way that the public views connections between crime and economy.
Accounts of youth crime and justice that are fostered in the media focus

almost exclusively on individual conduct and rarely on the criminogenic effect of the partnership between corporate capitalism and the state. The following section illustrates how a moral panic about children and crime arises in a modern political-economic context and how and why the media fosters images of criminalized children.

The Media and the Politics of Morality

Moral panics are characterized by their affiliations with politics, with systems of information and with institutions of social control, including the legal system. The operation of the moral panic is both symbolic and practical, and functions within the confines of an already existing orthodox state machinery that is closely tied to the mechanisms of production. And, most importantly for this chapter, moral panics are constituted within a discourse that has a profound effect on public opinion and on justifying punishment as a legitimate, moral form of social control. In the end, moral panics both drive public policy and are driven by policy decisions that, in part, respond to the "democratic will."

The Symbolic Crusade

Most youth-focused moral panics argue either to protect children or to condemn them. Constant warnings that children are in danger lead to lobbies against child abuse, child pornography, prostitution, paedophilia, serial killers, smoking and drunk driving. On the other hand, those who believe that all children are potentially dangerous have lobbied for the reform of the *Young Offenders Act*, implementation of dangerous offender legislation, the public security provisions of the *Youth Criminal Justice Act* and increased use of custodial dispositions for young offenders. Pessimism about and distrust of children are apparent in many news articles. Our ambivalence between protecting and condemning children is embodied in our cultural approach to child rearing, which advocates both affection/protection and physical punishment. Further, it is ironic that we tend to punish those who are both most dear to us, our children, and those who are farthest removed from us, the hardened criminal — the former inside our homes, the latter by incarceration.

The growing focus on criminogenic children and delinquent youth tends to divert public debate away from the political actions of the powerful that create social stresses for the less powerful (e.g., unemployment, welfare cuts, dangerous work environments, poorly paid and part-time labour). In addition, child-focused panics seem to set the limits of social tolerance and seek to change the moral and legal environment to reflect those limits. While harm to children is the threshold of tolerance, child-centred, symbolic lobbies reflect the belief that children are also unpredictable and volatile as a subculture. The attendant rhetoric invokes images of gangs and connections between nihilistic behaviour and music/dress (grunge as a typical example). The youth subculture is, in general, portrayed as aimless and calculating. The anti-youth lobby is a potent symbolic mechanism for framing youth crime — and ultimately all conduct — in ambivalent yet moralistic terms.

The Interdependence of Panics

Moral panics tend to emerge in groups and foster one another. The current movements in Canada directed against gun control, the drug trade, gang violence, car theft and dangerous offenders all make reference to youth involvement. Highly sensational incidents are interpreted as part of an overall social menace, and subsequent events are contextualized in this gestalt of fear and framed in fear-provoking language. The success of one panic lends credibility to another, and the result is a generalized lobby for increased social control at all levels. For example, when issues of youth crime and violence predominate on the airwaves, there are usually concurrent discussions of teen sexuality, youth prostitution and unwed motherhood. Issues of youth exploitation and disadvantage, then, become linked, by temporal association, to issues of youth menace and dangerousness, resulting in a generalized "problem of youth." The lumping together of adolescent issues transforms a problem that originates with the structure of society to one that appears to originate with youth themselves. The state and the adult world are absolved from responsibility for the exploitation of children and the social disadvantages that delinquent children represent.

The Role of the Mass Media

The North American newspaper and television industries seem to be continually moving toward monopolization by a few major media corporations. In effect, there is very little competition for the moral attention of Canadians and Americans. When I wrote the first edition of this book, Conrad Black, who at that time owned forty or more newspapers around the world, had purchased the four major daily newspapers in the province of Saskatchewan. And, in typical corporate rationalization, the company immediately laid off one quarter of the newspaper employees in the province. Since then, the Hollinger empire has sold its assets to another major Canadian newspaper conglomerate, CanWest Global, which owns 50 percent of the *National Post*, twenty-six other daily newspapers in Canada and television stations in the cities in which these newspaper are located. CanWest, along with other multi-national companies, including Rogers Media, Shaw Communications and Bell Canada, manage significant control of

Canadian airwaves, and as dynamic and aggressive corporations, they have a tremendous influence on the editorial slant of major social phenomena. They do this, in part, as a result of horizontal convergence with other media forms. This "cross media ownership" entails the corporate integration of information, entertainment and retail companies. As Brownlee shows, from 1999 onward in Canada, "all but one of the major English-Canada newspapers was the property of a TV or communications giant," and the unimpeachable reality is that "Canada's largest media corporations are heavily interlocked with other dominant Canadian corporations" (Brownlee 2005: 44).

The fundamental problem in all this is that journalistic integrity and balanced public commentary suffer. As the Southern Ontario Newspaper Guild asked: "How can there be credible democratic discourse in Canada or any country when the major public information channels, television and newspapers are owned or controlled by a handful of individuals accountable only to themselves?" (Southern Ontario Newspaper Guild 2005)

The Communications, Energy and Paperworkers of Canada (cep) have recently launched an effort to return journalistic integrity to Canadian news media. Their policy package includes "public editor's contracts, media advisory councils, limits on ownership within each medium, and a ban on cross-ownership between legitimate private interests and the public interest" (Southern Ontario Newspaper Guild 2005: 1). The thrust of this lobby is to subject media owners, managers and journalists to formal public scrutiny and collective and personal accountability. This is an interesting and important grassroots movement that, unfortunately, may whither and die in a global context of neo-liberalism and unbridled free enterprise.

Herman and Chomsky (1988) argued several years ago that media of all kinds are becoming increasingly concentrated in the hands of fewer and fewer large corporations. As the media come to be more and more connected to the corporate world, the deregulated market provides opportunities for corporate takeovers of small companies. Further, the fundamental focus on profit — redefined as allegiance to stockholders — takes priority over objective, fair and factual journalism. Concurrent with the devastating effect on the newspaper labour market, as the analysis in this book illustrates, the newspaper industry's passion for profit results in the production of sensationalist, often uncontested, news accounts that appear fictitious and largely removed from the social and economic context in which they occur, but which are highly marketable. I discuss media presentations at length in a subsequent section, but I wish to iterate at this point that the primary functions of media portraits of crime include: (a) the creation of a world of insiders and outsiders, acceptability and unacceptability in order to facilitate public demand and consumption; (b) the connecting of images of deviance and crime with social characteristics; and (c) the decontextualization of crime in anecdotal evidence, which is presented as omnipresent, non-complex truth.

The Interdependence of Institutions

Moral crusades are often typified by the collaboration of institutions of social control. On the issue of youth permissiveness, it is important to realize that institutions such as medicine, education, social welfare, religion and government are all involved in the work of understanding and controlling youth crime. It is not surprising, then, that public accounts of specific youth crimes, or of the youth crime epidemic generally, draw on experts from these institutions to lend credibility to their claims and to persuade audiences that the concern for growing youth crime is legitimate and widespread. And, politicians are quick to adopt a punitive stance toward youth, especially on behalf of conservative business and community leaders. As we will see, the interdependent and multi-institutional nature of moral panics is an important focus for the critical researcher in uncovering the claims to moral legitimacy that are made in public discourse and to revealing the actors who benefit from such claims.

Conclusion

As a sociological work, this book takes as its mission to place the moral panic against youth in an explanatory framework. The area of youth crime and justice has been inundated with a multitude of critical and consensus theories that have attempted to understand why youth choose to break the law or how a society is responsible for creating the conditions under which young people will end up at odds with that society. Conventional, consensus theories of youth crime especially predominate in the research and academic worlds. As they focus on the individual or cultural origins of crime and the ways to "correct" the offender, they support and foster the public's growing belief that youth are more disrespectful now than in the past, are more anti-social, especially towards adults, and ultimately are more dangerous. The policy implication of this "paradigm of panic" is to increase crime control and incarceration. And, this is no more evident than in the Canadian government's crime bill — one of the five platforms of Stephen Harper's new conservative government — which is based on increased re-active policing, standardized and harsh sentencing, and increased use of incarceration for youth and adults. In contrast, and hopefully as an antidote to regressive and consequently oppressive, justice strategies, the orientation of this book is both critical and social constructionist. The critical position draws on the debates surrounding the concept of the moral panic in the late sixties and early seventies. The corpus of that work attempted to unpack the hidden agenda behind the creation of a mythology of delinquency. In this book, I accept the challenge of that mythology, as well. I discuss the advantages that accrue to the influential players in this public debate, how they construct and produce images of deviance that absolve them from responsibility for social conditions and indict others who are less powerful, and how constructed images of good and evil infiltrate the public consciousness to the degree that young people are excluded from the common good. This book is essentially a study of ideology, of a collective belief system that constricts the way we see the world, especially with respect to issues of good and evil. Ultimately, such a belief system ties the morality of good and evil to socio-economic characteristics.

The social constructionist approach presumes that knowledge (social or natural facts) is largely created, most often for a political purpose. Even the most objective-based knowledge is relative to time and place, and professionals/experts who are charged with understanding criminality are powerful constructors of portraits of crime. Discourse, knowledge and power are inextricably connected in a paradigm that awakens us to the need to deconstruct official and public opinions. Those who make claims to truth, and who often get their perceptions of reality translated into public opinion and public policy, are most often in positions of political and economic power. They have considerable ability to persuade the public that a condition exists and that it presents a threat to public security. I argue throughout this book that the ongoing moral panic surrounding youth crime is a typical example of a constructed social problem: the objective threat is much less than the collective public sentiment would hold to be true. In addition, and most importantly, the powerful, economically advantaged members of our society gain considerable advantage by fostering a moral panic surrounding youth crime and dangerousness.

Overall, the sociological sensitivity to young offenders is important in unpacking the forces that would at once blame children for social ills and at the same time denounce anyone who would endanger children. I believe that this contradictory and unnerving posture towards Canada's youth can only be understood within a political-economic framework that poses the following question: If children are our most cherished resource, why then do we denounce and fear adolescence and ultimately discard children for political and moral ends?

CHAPTER 2

Understanding Child-Hating

There are two theoretical approaches that inform this book. The first falls under the broad rubric of social constructionism and assumes that public images of acceptable behaviour and the appropriate penalties for violations of social norms are highly variable, as is the definition of "normal" behaviour. As a result, what constitutes unacceptable behaviour changes over time and across social groups and societies. The social construction approach is informed largely by historical studies that track changing modes of social control. As we observe the public and political venom that is directed towards children and youth and as we think about youth misconduct in relation to the structure, culture and family of contemporary society, we are left with the gnawing question: "What is going on?" It is almost axiomatic that moral panics occur in troubled times. Our focus is on how power operates in defining and sanctioning virtuous and evil behaviour amongst youth.

The second theoretical concern attempts to understand the origins and intent of such power. The presumption is that fear, in its collective manifestation, becomes highly politicized as it is manipulated either inadvertently or deliberately for political and economic ends. This political economy/critical dimension of the theoretical framework, derived from Marxist philosophical principles, focuses on the structure of the society and, specifically, on the relationship between the media and the powerful sectors of the society. The presumption is that those in control of the economy manage to have their ideas transformed into general notions of morality and crime. They reproduce notions that become generalized belief systems, the bases of our ideology. The main presumption in this ideology is that some people are better than others by virtue of their place in the socio-economic structure of the society and that they have "merited" their advantage. The discourse of meritocracy and the attendant defamation of those who are dispossessed and marginalized are powerful mechanisms for legitimating a highly stratified society. As I mentioned at the end of the previous chapter, such an ideology serves to reproduce class relations by constraining the way that we think about issues of goodness and badness and their connection to poverty and wealth. The defamation of social groups through the discourse of crime and punishment is a powerful political mechanism.

In chapter one, I presented a social, legal and historical discussion for understanding Canada's current moral panic about youth, and in light of the two theoretical orientations above, I return to those specific positions to make sense of the paradoxical connection between child victimization and child blaming. I must also state that many youths who suffer economic, social and personal privation go on to become law-abiding and productive citizens. And, of course, much of the rhetoric of law and order is based on the presumption that everybody at one time or another has suffered victimization but only the truly bad engage in criminal behaviour. The theoretical sociological positions I address in this book ask how a stratified society not only creates criminal behaviour, but constructs certain types of behaviour and persons as unacceptable, not on the basis of an inherent morality, but rather on the basis of social signifiers.

The Sociology of Knowledge and the Deconstruction of Crime Myth

Fear and the knowledge that underpins that fear are important foci for this book. We are forced, as social analysts, to confront the task of deconstructing public opinion that we assume to be based on selected and biased knowledge. Further, we need to uncover the sources of information and assess the claims to legitimacy — or in journalistic parlance, the claims to objectivity — that inform and direct public opinion. Cohen (1980) has made us aware that public opinion fluctuates and that it may cause social reform:

> Societies appear to be subject, every now and then, to periods of moral panic. A condition, episode, person or group of persons emerges to become defined as a threat to societal values and interests: its nature is presented in a stylized and stereo-typical fashion by the mass media: the moral barricades are manned by editors, bishops, politicians and other right-thinking people; socially accredited experts pronounce their diagnoses and solutions…. Sometimes the panic is passed over and is forgotten, except in folklore and collective memory; at other times it has more serious and long lasting repercussions and might produce such changes as those in legal and social policy or even in the way society conceives itself. (28)

The information contained in this book, gleaned from multiple media sources, identifies many of the characteristics of a typical moral panic. The massive and biased coverage of Canada's youth criminals and pre-criminals by the press and by politicians bears witness to the stability, persistence and power of a war against youth crime. Social constructionism, as part of the domain of post-modernism, is based on the methodological position that "deconstruction tears a text (all phenomena, all events, are texts) apart, reveals its contradictions and assumptions" (Rosenau 1992). We need to ask the following questions:

- What are the hidden messages that "objective journalism" conveys?
- Who are the originators of such ideological communiqués?
- How do these originators make claims to legitimacy?
- Who are the expressed and insinuated targets of the social/political attack?

From the discussions in Chapters 4, 5 and 6, it will become clear that the recurring focus in media and political accounts of youth crime are people who live on the margins. The manifest messages are that society is too lenient with children and that the only way to restore order and appropriate conduct is to become "tough" through law and order. The associated belief is that kids are inherently evil and that discipline and punishment are essential in the creation of normal, law-abiding children. The latent messages are much more damning. Youths who break laws belong to certain racial and ethnic categories, they are born and raised in the lower socio-economic strata of the society, their families are feminized, and their lack of morality stems from their socio-economic positions in society. Simply put, the messages indict poverty and endorse wealth, blame the poor for being poor, condemn mothers almost exclusively for poor parenting and censure cultural difference as criminogenic.

The work of Michel Foucault is particularly instructive in understanding the nature of discourse surrounding young offenders. For Foucault, discourses are

> historically variable ways of specifying knowledge and truth — what it is possible to speak of at a given moment. They function (especially scientific discourses) as sets of rules, and the operation of these rules and concepts in programmes which specify what is or is not the case — what constitutes insanity, for example. Discourses are, therefore, powerful. Those who are labelled insane, or hysterical women or frigid wives, are in the grip of power. This power may be exercised by officials through institutions, or through many other practices, but power is constituted in discourses and it is in discourses, such as those in clinical medicine, that power lies. Discourses produce truths and "we cannot exercise power except through the production of truth" (Foucault, in Ramazanoglu 1993: 10)

Foucault argues that historical periods are marked by particular discourses that constrain the types of knowledge that are produced. Knowledge is constructed and deployed on the basis of what types of people have access to the systems of knowledge, and it is this access to "legitimate knowledge" that gives people their power.

The basic tenets of a Foucauldian power/knowledge perspective are quite evident in the discourse of youth offenders. The ways of speaking about young offenders are restricted largely to individual or family-based accounts of the origins of crime. Rarely are the explanations based on structural inequalities or the injustice of people living on the margins of society. As Foucault has suggested, the discourses of historical periods are constrictive; they are rules under which "talk" can be carried out. The modern discourse of youth crime and punishment appear to be restricted to accounts based on individual blame. This contemporary medical/psychological discourse of goodness and badness sets youth crime in a context of orthodox criminology: individuals gone wrong, either inherently or culturally. The underlying ideological position is that society is structured correctly and that individuals who offend are individually or socially pathological and identifiable.

The discourse of individual or cultural blame receives its legitimacy primarily through the knowledge of experts. The language and accounts of youth criminality are often the products of testimonials by "scientists." Discourse operates as a powerful and oppressing mechanism, because it comes from the mouths of "legitimated speakers," who are almost without exception drawn from the privileged sectors of society. As the analysis of media accounts in this book shows, news articles are often infused with the voices of "professionals," who corroborate the claims made in the article. This strategy not only endorses the validity of the account, it also gives the media legitimacy by association. Furthermore, the "expert wisdom" of legitimated speakers is often accompanied by the folk wisdom of "ordinary people" and it is this technique of attaching common knowledge to expert knowledge that produces a generalized atmosphere of credibility.

In his treatises on power and knowledge, Foucault was generally unconcerned with the origins of discourses and what interests they served. Typical of post-modern orientations, his approach to the study of the social construction of truth focuses on how power and knowledge operate, not on what discourses mean, but rather on what makes them possible. This approach leaves us with the crucial questions of who controls the images of youth, who benefits from biased and incriminating portraits of offenders and why certain categories of people are the targets of journalistic and political abuse. To answer these questions we need to turn to the critical feminist and political economy-based theories of knowledge as it relates to criminality, and we need to harvest such theories for insights into and responses to the rhetoric of child-hating.

Feminist Theory and the Construction of Gendered Images

Law-amd-order campaigns are also veiled attacks on women and feminism. Media presentations maintain that women are susceptible to victimization and poverty more so than men, but that they also, through their inadequate parenting, are the producers of criminality. In essence, women are the inadvertent victimizers of children. Such stereotypical and conventional explanations of criminality have focused on non-traditional families, non-traditional motherhood, single-parenthood and poverty as causal factors in youth criminality. Feminist responses to the conservative, traditional explanations of crime are that patriarchal ideologies frame the nature of women's crime and the imputed female role in criminogenesis. While feminism, as a generic theoretical position, is highly complex and multi-dimensional, feminist studies in general address the structure of society as disadvantageous to women: in hierarchical societies, men generally inhabit positions of privilege and domination over women. In such societies, women and men live in different experiential worlds, but the knowledge that underpins our understanding of gender issues is largely produced by men and is based on stereotypical and distorted ideas about women and men. And, importantly for this book, these stereotypical "sexist" images that connect maternity and motherhood to criminality are reproduced in the media. As Anderson suggests,

> Although these institutions are not the exclusive sources of sexist ideas, they exert a powerful influence on the way we define reality and women's role within it…. In fact, it can be argued that in a highly complex technological-industrial society, these systems of communication and knowledge making play an increasingly important part in the generation and transmission of ideas…. Moreover, as the feminist movement has shown, images of women conveyed by the media and in educational materials have been based on distortions and stereotypes that legitimate the status quo at the same time that they falsely represent the actual experience of women in the society. Thus, the ideas we acquire regarding gender relations poorly prepare us for the realities we will face. (1988: 25)

Public images of typical delinquents are primarily about males. When female youth are targeted, the depictions are couched in "paradox talk": it is so unusual for girls to act aggressively or anti-socially that bad genes must be at work. The "sugar and spice" understanding of femaleness is often the standard upon which young female offenders are judged, and the images of "bad girls" are presented as biological anomalies and/or the sinister products of the feminist movement. A general women-hatred appears to underlie the "sugar and spice" conception of femaleness in articles that discuss the wild, passionate, out-of-character woman who has to be constrained or held back always: a dual stereotype of women in western society — she is nice but emotional and unpredictable.

The second way that women are included and loathed in media accounts of youth crime is through speculations about the causal origins of delinquent behaviour. Specifically, the references are to "feminist women" trying to be more like men or to the inability of single mothers to raise "normal children" in the confines of the "abnormal family" living in conditions of privation. In the United States, much ink has been spent on fatherlessness, especially for black youth, who constitute the largest percentage of criminalized and incarcerated young people (Daniels 1998). The basic presumption in the collected works that comprise Cynthia Daniels' book is that conservative political and social pundits blame the criminogenesis of black youth on absentee fathers and by association, single mothers:

> the collapse of children's well-being in the United States has reached breathtaking proportions. Juvenile crime has increased six-fold.... One can think of many explanations for these unhappy developments.... But the evidence is now strong that the absence of fathers from the lives of children is one of the most important causes.... The proliferation of mother-headed families now constitutes something of a national economic emergency. (Popenoe 1998: 37).

The "family values" reference that has become so much a part of the conservative political creed is infused with references to the functional two-parent heterosexual family and the importance of male discipline and male role models. In contradistinction to public opinion and media hype, however, empirical evidence on street youth and youth who have been in contact with the courts indicates that single-parenthood shows little correlation with law-breaking behaviour. More to the point, living a life of poverty, which is often typical for single mothers, is a predisposing condition to contact with the law. Problems resulting from structural inequality and the unfairness of a market-based economy are transposed to problems of mothering and ultimately to problems created by feminism.

A feminist approach to studying the social construction of public knowledge is important for locating the sources of bias against women in the patriarchal structures that support media, politics, academia/education and the economy. As evidenced by the analysis in this book, condemnatory images of women are created and deployed in a rhetoric of fear, inherent criminality and unnatural predispositions. The constructed and gendered knowledge about youth crime originates in patriarchal political and economic systems. As the following section discusses, the fundamental issue in a critical analysis of social phenomena is that some people dominate others by virtue of their position of advantage in the political and economic structure, and that state policy is either directly or indirectly complicit in the system of domination and subordination.

Ideology, Power, and the Images of Youth

The theoretical orientation that directly addresses the issues of domination by powerful people over less powerful people as a primary focus can be subsumed under the broad category of Marxist (sometimes called, conflict) criminology. The primary assumption in Marxist-based theories is that certain groups of people gain advantage over others and dominate by virtue of their position of privilege and ownership in the system of production. In the context of this book we are concerned with understanding the creators of images of youth and those who are advantaged and disadvantaged by the social construction of knowledge. It is important to understand issues of power and economy in a contemporary context; the arguments I make in *Still Blaming Children* have to be placed in a context in which neo-liberal fiscal and social policies frame global politics.

As I have stated, global economics dictates constraints on government spending, which erodes the state's ability to provide for its citizens. The welfare and the civil liberties of the most vulnerable citizens become jeopardized. Canadian youth, as a formally disenfranchised group, are threatened most certainly by governmental policy, which promotes business group interests at the expense of social programs. In essence, business has the implicit right to set the social agenda (Bourdieu 1999; Giroux 2003b). Males (2000) has argued that the baby boom generation, either through pension plans or through direct investments, has a profound interest in protecting its financial legacy and it does so by ensuring that social programs that support young people do not drain its collective resources. I argue, in addition, that young people bolster the economy to their own detriment as they provide cheap, unsecured labour and are targeted as vulnerable consumers. One of the basic arguments in this book is that the negative portraits of youth culture that occur in the news media serve an important function for business interests. If the general public views youth as dangerous and criminal they are less likely to be sympathetic to the increasingly dire economic situation that today's youth face and, are most likely to favour "law-amd-order" approaches to youth misconduct rather than "social investment" approaches. The control of the media serves an extremely important legitimation function for business: through the media's sensationalist reporting, the general public comes to believe that the bad things that happen are the result of individual badness and not the result of social inequality and dispossession. The relationship between poverty levels and youth crime disappears from public discourse and is replaced with portraits of youth who are lazy, unwilling to work, immoral and criminally volatile.

The instrumental Marxist argument (Quinney 1974; Goff and Reasons 1978) has suggested that powerful people directly influence government policy and manipulate such policy to their advantage. Government is government for the wealthy and powerful. This understanding of power and corporate control of politics is somewhat difficult to envision in societies based on the democratic process. However, as nation states lose their autonomy to manage public spending through dictates from lending institutions like the World Bank and the International Monetary Fund and through trade agreements like the World Trade Organization, one could easily make the argument that powerful business interests do, in fact, dictate public policy. Nations that invest in public spending become "bad economic risks" (Bourdieu 1999; Carroll 2004; Robbins 2005).

The structural Marxist approach (Poulantzas 1972; Balbus 1973), on the other hand, allows for the reality that ordinary people, through the democratic process, can resist the neo-liberal world of global capital. The overall approach argues that the state is relatively autonomous from the power brokers, but that the role of the state is to create and maintain the conditions under which capital accumulation works most efficiently, e.g., by putting a cap on spending on social programs. In so doing, the state must create the conditions under which the system of capital accumulation is held legitimate by the populace. Otherwise the democratic process would likely dictate the end of a system based on such domination and subordination. It is at this point where the question of the ideological role of the media needs to be raised:

> The media, then, do not simply "create" the news; nor do they simply transmit the ideology of the "ruling class" in a conspiratorial fashion. Indeed, we have suggested, in a critical sense, the media are frequently not the "primary definers" of news events at all; but their structured relationship to power has the effect of

making them play a crucial but secondary role in reproducing the definitions of those who have privileged access, as of right, to the media as "accredited sources." (Hall et al. 1978: 59)

Hall and his colleagues took this structural Marxist position and applied it to the moral panics surrounding "mugging" in England in the 1960s and 1970s. They illustrated how the raw materials of crime facts get filtered to the media and are produced as "factual" stories, which ultimately serve to reproduce the ideologies of powerful people.

In this book, I illustrate how stereotypical images of race, class and gender are created and employed to produce versions of goodness and badness attributable to class position. The obvious question is why news definers and makers conform to the dominant ideology of a modern day "ruling class," especially when the professed mandate of the media is objectivity and journalistic integrity.

Ownership

Observation of the ownership patterns of the Canadian news media reveals that newspapers and newsmagazines are monopolized by a few major corporate interests. As mentioned in Chapter 1, CanWest Global owns 50 percent of the *National Post*, twenty-six other daily newspapers in Canada and television stations in the cities in which these newspaper are located. CanWest, along with other large media corporations, including Rogers Media, Shaw Communications and Bell Canada, control a significant amount of Canada's airwaves (Brownlee 2005; Southern Ontario Newspaper Guild 2005). These aggressive and successful corporations have incredible influence on the editorial slant of Canadian social phenomena, with the result that journalistic freedom and balanced public commentary suffer. The arguments of Herman and Chomsky (1988) regarding media concentration and relatively simple regarding the loss of journalistic integrity. The fundamental focus on profit and the associated corporate agenda to control editorial policy dictate that journalistic accounts cannot be balanced. Corporate allegiance to stockholders takes priority over objective, fair and factual journalism. Through a variety of daily and mundane mechanisms (most of them indirect), a converging corporate domination and monopolization of the news creates narrowed comprehension and tolerance for issues that involve disaffiliated and marginalized peoples. John McMullen provides a poignant example of the corporate influence in the making of a news story. In *News, Truth and Crime* (2005), he describes the media focus on the human tragedy of the Westray mining disaster in Nova Scotia in 1992 and how the singular and unrelenting focus on the lives lost and the families disrupted diverted attention from the corporate lawlessness and state complicity in the explosion, the subsequent inaction and the cover up (McMullan 2005).

The influence that corporations have on the nature and content of journalism is enhanced by the tenuous nature of journalists' jobs. The threat of dismissal is a powerful compulsion for reporters to toe the corporate line, and this has certainly never been more true than after 9/11, when American reporters either lost or were threatened with losing their jobs for "non-party-line" reporting (Chomsky 2002). The controlled images are still produced in a framework of journalism and appear as objective, "factual" accounts of the social condition. The constructed images of goodness and badness that we see in media portraits of young offenders, for example, become the bases of the moral framework for the entire society.

Credibility

The legitimacy of the created moral framework is maintained not only by the ownership of the news but also by the credibility of the news. Only certain types of individuals are credited with the ability to comment on issues of badness and goodness. And, it is no coincidence that the primary commentators in news reports are generally professional, highly educated people who are obviously highly placed in the socio-economic system. As we will see in Chapters 4, 5 and 6, accounts that speculate on the causes of youth crime are created and endorsed by judges, lawyers, police officers, university professors, doctors and business owners. The credibility of these people results largely from their assumed superior knowledge and their links to science, in this case forensic and legal science. Part of their appeal is their unique access to the exclusive languages of law and science, which, to an uninitiated public, seems mystical, inaccessible and by definition, correct. It is no coincidence that the legitimate speakers are drawn from the higher echelons of society. Much of their understanding of crime and punishment, as a result, is based on the values and morals of privilege. Marx's aphorism that "the ruling ideas of any age are the ideas of its ruling class" is especially apt when we consider the socio-economic origins of "legitimate experts." Rarely are media accounts based on the insights and knowledge of marginalized or underclass people. Interestingly, the use of subverted knowledge is not an impossibility. As I show in the final chapter in this book, in a rare instance in which a crime account was presented through the eyes of a young street person, the vision was especially poignant and as relevant as any so-called expert opinion that we have analyzed.

Process

The final method through which the ideas of dominant people get translated into dominating ideas is through selective media attention. Hall et al. (1978) argue that not every statement by a relevant primary definer in respect of a particular topic is likely to be reproduced in the media; nor is every part of each statement. By exercising selectivity the media begin to impose their own criteria on the structured "raw materials" — and thus actively appropriate and transform them... the criteria of selection — a mixture of professional, technical and commercial constraints — serves to orientate the media in general to the "definitions of the powerful." (60)

On this point, I agree with Hall et al., and the work in this book lends support to their thesis. The authors, however, go on to state that

each paper's professional sense of the newsworthy, its organization and technical framework (in terms of numbers of journalists working in particular new areas, amount of column space routinely given over to certain kinds of news items, and so on), and sense of audience or regular readers, is different. Such differences, taken together, are what produce the very different "social personalities of papers." (60)

On this point my analysis departs from the work of Hall and his associates. As I argue throughout this book, the stories, the visual and verbal images, and the scientific accounts of youth crime are remarkably similar and constructed around a rigid set of journalistic/ideological rules. The newspapers and newsmagazines, with some differences in the extent of inflammatory rhetoric, could be interchanged quite easily, with little change in content or intent. Hall et al. (1978) do concede that despite the different languages of newspapers, the accounts occur within certain ideological constraints. I would add that the constraints are so strong that the languages are one and the same.

Theoretical Synthesis

Overall, the Marxist and feminist perspectives allow us to understand the entire moral panic against youth in the context of power and social control. As Box argues, crime and criminalization are social control strategies in that they:

(i) render underprivileged and powerless people more likely to be arrested, convicted, and sentenced to prison, even though the amount of personal damage and injury they cause may be less than the more powerful and privileged cause; (ii) create the illu-

> sion that the "dangerous" class is primarily located at the bottom of various hierarchies by which we "measure" each other, such as occupational prestige, income level, housing market location, educational achievement, racial attributes — in this illusion it fuses relative poverty and criminal propensities and sees them both as effects of moral inferiority, thus rendering the "dangerous" class deserving of both poverty and punishment. (1983: 13)

That images of poverty align with immorality and badness is manifest in media constructions, and the political economy-based moral panic literature is essential in understanding the origins of hate. What is less obvious, however, are the mechanisms through which racial minorities, women and poor people get reframed in the public's mind from people who lack privilege to people who are dangerous. Post-modern theoretical and methodological bases for unpacking commonsense language as the language of politics help us round out a theory of social constructionism of child-hating.

These theoretical positions help us understand a fundamental truth about crime, the news and the economy: when the general population is preoccupied with (and terrified of) street crime, the economic and social problems that disenfranchised people face virtually disappear from their consciousness. The construction and perpetuation of crime panics of any nature serve to pervade the consciousness of ordinary people, convincing them that street crime is the most imminent problem facing the society. The problems that our political economy has created — unemployment, the silencing of labour, record profits for major corporations at the expense of jobs (the Canadian banks exemplify this quite clearly), the continuing trend toward monopoly capitalism, decreased proportionate spending on health, education and welfare and a growing disenchantment with politics and politicians — become of marginal importance in the consciousness of the average Canadian when crime, criminals and lenient justice are the primary horror stories in the news. The effect of this "false consciousness" is that powerful people carry on with "business as usual," with little or no opposition from the general public. Many ordinary citizens, convinced that all social evils stem from bad economies, support conservative fiscal and social policies even during bad times. This study of the construction and management of a moral panic against youth helps us understand how institutions like the economy, law and politics maintain their legitimacy in light of clear evidence that they are largely responsible for a widening gap between the rich and the poor and for a growing underclass in North America. That ordinary people, including those of marginalized and oppressed classes, "buy into" arguments that we are at peril from street criminals and not the global economic activity of the privileged, suggests that hegemony works very effectively through the news media.

The Place of Children and Youth in the Global Economy

One of the difficulties in attempting to understand the exploitation of children and youth in the modern world is that we really do not have a sense of where young people fit in the continuum between work and play. Common sense and scientific evidence suggest that children and adolescents need to grow and develop in a protected world in which they can learn from their mistakes. Social convention suggests that young people are not to be exploited in any way, but that they should be involved in civic participation as a training ground for citizenship. Childhood and adolescence, then, are times for freedom from mental and physical trauma.

The reality, however, is very much dissonant with the perception. In many global contexts, children and youth have very little chance to develop without trauma. In the developing world, children and youth are exposed to war, sexual exploitation, disease and privation in unprecedented proportions (cf. Morris 1995; Newman 2000; O'Higgins 2001; International Labour Organization (ILO) 2002). In the developed world, children and youth are similarly exposed to trauma, albeit in a more subtle or concealed fashion. They are exploited in the labour market, with little access to the human rights that accrue to adults (cf. Reiter 1996; Glor 1989; ILO 2004; Basran, Gill and MacLean 1995; Human Rights Watch (HRW) 2000). They are exploited by merchandising industries that prey on the culture of youth (cf. Milner Jr. 2004; Sutherland and Thompson 2003). They are exploited in the sports arena, where fun is replaced by militaristic discipline in the guise of perfection and teamwork (cf. Robinson 1998; Miedzian 1998). They are exploited by the industry of medicine, in which "child" pathologies are a new breeding ground for medical research (cf. Green and Healy 2003; Diller 1998), and they are exploited in war, in which young people fight while older people sit in safety and watch (cf. Bourke 1999; Grossman 1995; Edelman 1985). And for children and youth in both developed and developing worlds, their exploitation occurs primarily in a political context in which they have virtually no input into what happens to them. If a portion of the population does not have the opportunity to engage in civic and political participation (at more than a superficial level) and if that population is exploited for their labour and for their consumption, what results is a modern form of slavery. Young people are indentured labourers, involuntary soldiers, guinea pigs for medical and pharmaceutical research, and victims of human trafficking for sexual and commercial exploitation.

If this is true, how we have come to a point where we accept the deceit that children and youth are our most valuable asset.

The basic thesis of this chapter, and this book in general, is that systems of public discourse, like news media, frame the way the general public thinks about social issues and that, with reference to children and youth, the framework is largely condemnatory. The basic question is why that should be. The answer lies with an understanding of the correlation between global corporatism and the condemnation of children and youth, accomplished in part through a punitive youth justice policy and a concomitant public discourse about dangerous young people. Essentially, the global context is one in which social policy and public discourse create the conditions under which children and youth lose their civil liberties to the vagaries and demands of global capital (Grossberg 2005). The global context in which public policy tends increasingly to condemn and marginalize youth is characterized by two aforementioned incontrovertible phenomena: the growing involvement of children and youth in a labour market — including the use of children and youth in the military — that provides low wage; poor working conditions and a denial of the rights and freedoms accorded to working adults; and the positioning of children and youth as super-consumers in both the developed and developing worlds. In Chapter 3, I take up these issues in some detail.

To understand subjugation and exploitation of any kind, we need to understand how the discourse that legitimates exploitation evolves, becomes dispersed and takes on a peculiarly commonsense quality. To understand the "common sense" about children and youth, we need to look to institutions, particularly crime/justice and the media. Youth justice systems in Canada and the United States are particularly harsh. The public's perception of "criminal" youth and the magnitude of youth criminality come primarily through popular cultural depictions of youth crime, many of which are contained in so-called objective, journalistic contexts. As we will observe in the next four chapters, journalistic accounts have the potential to be extremely damaging to the image of youth. Common-sense perceptions about youth crime, however negative and unfounded, buttress a system of justice that is harsh, non-rehabilitative and ultimately supportive of the global exploitation of children and youth. In short, the ideological power of media (both fictional and non-fictional) fosters a context in which children are seen as incompletely developed non-citizens. Their exploitation, therefore, is implicitly justifiable. This is especially ironic in the developed world, in which human rights are ostensibly the most well-preserved.

CHAPTER 3

Actors in the Theatre of Crime

The theatrical depiction of public panics in this book is a deliberate metaphor; it is intended to emphasize the fictional, constructed nature of events presumed to be factual and to illustrate that the consumer/reader is compelled or at least invited to empathize with the victim or the hero who solves the problem.

As with most issues involving public opinion, the majority of players in the drama benefit and are distinguishable by their degree of self-interest and volition. These beneficiaries are the direct and indirect authors of the fiction. In general, beneficiaries gain economic, political, cultural or moral advantage from portraits that are intended to distance the creators from the protagonists. In the context of the current panic over youth crime, the beneficiaries are myriad but interrelated and include everyone but the victim and the young person as folk devil.

The Press

If we accept for the moment Marshall McLuhan's aphorism that "the medium is the message," then we also must accept his contention that "the owners of media always endeavour to give the public what it wants, because they sense that their power is in the *medium* and not in the *message* or the program" (McLuhan 1964: 193). This suggests several things: that media producers give us what they think we want to hear and not necessarily the facts; that the television, radio and print media are so ambient that they are "staples or natural resources, exactly as are coal and cotton and oil.... That our human senses, of which all media are extensions... configure the awareness and experience of each one of us" (McLuhan 1964: 35). The media have the power to construct slanted or fictional accounts of real life incidents by decontextualizing and simplifying the news. The resulting binary depictions are presented as unambiguous accounts of good and evil, offering us, at best, supposedly what we want to hear, and at worst, all we are capable of understanding.

Kellner (1995) has warned us that as we live in a media and consumer society, we run the risk of passively accepting what we see and read without questioning the content or the moral message. He argues that the media is the consummate ideological tool.

Radio, television, film and the other products of media culture provide materials out of which we forge our very identities, our sense of selfhood; our notion of what it means to be male or female; our sense of class, of ethnicity and race, of nationality, of sexuality, of "us" and "them." Media images help shape our view of the world and our deepest values: what we consider good or bad, positive or negative, moral or evil. Media stories provide the symbols, myths and resources through which we constitute a common culture and through the appropriation of which we insert ourselves into this culture. Media spectacles demonstrate who has power and who is powerless, who is allowed to exercise force and violence and who is not. They dramatize and legitimate the power of the forces that be and show the powerless that they must stay in their places or be destroyed. (Kellner 1995: 5)

Ultimately, the media provides the discourse for understanding things that happen in the real world. Twenty years ago, Neil Postman argued that television is the modern medium that establishes the tools for viewing, reading and understanding:

We have reached, I believe, a critical mass in that electronic media have decisively and irreversibly changed the character of our symbolic environment. We are now a culture whose information, ideas and epistemology are given form by television, not by the printed word. To be sure, there are still readers and there are many books published, but the uses of print and reading are not the same as they once were; not even in schools, the last institutions where print was thought to be invincible. They delude themselves who believe that television and print coexist, for coexistence implies parity. There is no parity here. Print is now merely a residual epistemology, and it will remain so, aided to some extent by the computer, and newspapers and magazines that are made to look like television screens. (1985: 28)

The importance of seeing television as an epistemological device is manifest as a watershed period in human. Television makes it possible to ingest brief images of news without having to spend time doing so. The impact of the shortened attention span is that we are rendered unreceptive to contextualized accounts. For example, when we read oversized alarmist headlines or see pictures in magazines of kids wielding guns, these images often satiate our interest. Postman and others have argued that television has done this to us, that it has created a discourse of abbreviated images and messages from which we cannot escape. It is impossible, for example, to listen to hours-long political speeches today: in the past, public forum political debates were grand social events and the speakers held the audience's attention for hours. The last vestige of this in the Canadian political arena existed in the Diefenbaker/Pearson era in Canada and the Kennedy era in the U.S. These were probably the last professional orators; they gave way to the advent of the electronic media era and the shortened public attention span. In contemporary media, furthermore, long speeches do not fit into the demands of advertising. Even political debates are scheduled around advertising, and most political commentary is delivered in short sound bites that allow directors to control the pace and the size of the presentation to conform to the demands of advertising and scheduling.

I part company in this book with authors like Postman and McLuhan in that I contend that other types of media adjust to the discourse of visual media and become like a typographic television. Magazines, newspapers and now the Internet, use television techniques to sell their messages. The fundamental consideration in the age of television is that what we see and read must entertain. This has profound implications for the news media; its primary function, in competition for the attention of the viewing/seeing public, is to use journalistic "facts" in an entertaining context. And, this is what we see in modern news media accounts, some of which I analyze in this book. Because of the highly profitable nature of "the news," a vast and expanding body of discursive techniques has arisen, the most recent being the Internet, which permits access to international images and accounts in seconds. Much like the truncated portraits typical of television, the Internet news sources are necessarily brief, often accompanied by photographs and often unabashedly biased. But, we need look no farther than the grocery store check-out stand or magazine rack to see that the print medium has proliferated despite the ubiquity of television. Even within television, intense competition for the public's attention creates various forms of accounts, including docudramas, daytime talk shows (which purport to deal with real life issues), "true crime" shows (in which the camera follows law enforcement officials) and actual courtroom eavesdropping.

Despite this profusion of discursive vehicles, my focus in this book is on newspapers and newsmagazines, principally because these two media have not diminished but, I argue, have instead changed in form and content to compete in the electronic era. The use of the tabloid style of newspaper, typical of the SUN chain is an attempt to make the newspaper physically easier to handle on the bus, at the local coffee shop, or standing on the street corner, all situations that allow only brief periods of time to ingest the news. Magazines of all stripes, including newsmagazines, proliferate in the waiting rooms of public places — including the offices of doctors, dentists, mechanics, hairdressers and lawyers. Although these may appear to be banal examples of access to news discourse, I contend that the accounts found within the magazines reach a wide audience and are viewed in a very cursory way. The time span for viewing/reading is short and the visual images are the most influential components. Although I have no hard evidence regarding the degree of public exposure, I was recently struck by an experience that indicated to me the power of the magazine, even in relation to television. I entered a waiting room in a large automobile repair chain and sat amongst ten or eleven patrons waiting for their automobiles. A television was hanging in the corner of the room and a daytime soap was on. What interested me was that all of the individuals in the room were reading magazines and newspapers, only rarely glancing up to the images on the screen. While this is not a typical viewing situation, it does indicate, if only in an anecdotal way, the allure of the magazine and the newspaper, especially when time is limited.

What I am suggesting is that the print media are still profoundly influential. And importantly, with respect to the images of youth studied in this book, the photographs and the headlines are the things that the cursory reader sees and likely remembers. The short attention span of the modern reader is vulnerable to images that are necessarily simplistic and decontextualized. A television-based discourse provides "news" accounts of crime that can only be taken and understood out of context; crime becomes fiction.

The Epistemological Power of the News Media

To understand the phenomena of constructed crime, it is important to remember that the media responds to the pressure of supply and demand in producing news for mass consumption. This fact gains significance by the added twist that by creating sensationalist accounts of real life incidents, supposedly to appeal to the prurient desires in most readers/viewers, the media has exceptional political/ideological power. In the creation and promotion of sensationalist news accounts, the media creates a world of us and them, of insiders and outsiders, a world of fear. In so doing, the media embed stereotypical images of deviants and menaces on our collective psyches, which guide us as we form opinions about crime and punishment and make us wary of all kinds of "outsiders." Glassner (1999) shows us how a "culture of fear" arises in a popular cultural discourse in which the public comes to fear all kinds of contexts that are unfamiliar or unlike those in which they have experience. The outsider in popular culture, the ghetto youth as a prototypical example, are modern day folk devils whose images circumscribe the way we think about good and evil. Quite clearly, the role of the media in the creation of a fearful world is an important dimension of understanding why certain kinds of people come to be our "social enemies."

This position about the formative power of the media is more complex than I have stated. That the media has epistemological influence has been well-established over decades (McLuhan1964; Iyengar and Kinder 1987; Kellner 1995; Herman and Chomsky 1994; Roberts and Koehr 2004; Mc-Mullan 2005), but this argument stands in contradiction to those made by media economists, who contend that the media respond in a supply and demand manner to the wishes of the consumer. This supply and demand position tends to be somewhat banal in its implication that people democratically control what they see and how they understand what they see. Although I do not vehemently deny this position, I feel strongly that the panics and hatred that modern society has formed regarding young people are, at least in part, the results of constructed, controlled and decontextualized images of kids.

The generalized cultural fears and concerns that generated my writing of this book and its earlier incarnation are based on the media depictions of young criminals as the new folk devils, images that are biased in terms of gender, class and race/ethnicity. The following analysis of the print media is based on the hypothesis that the public's commonsense understandings of young criminals originate with fictionalized, distorted, stereotypical accounts of young offenders and their socio-economic affiliations, and that those who present these partial images have a two-dimensional vested interest, at once economic and ideological.

One of the fundamental tenets of a free press is that reporters are not constrained by any outside force to present the news in a particular way. Furthermore, the news reporter takes an implicit oath to report the facts objectively and without editorial bias. Marshal McLuhan first awakened us to the likelihood that the message that we receive is dependent on the medium and on those in positions of ownership. His admonition that the "medium is the message" (1964) was a forewarning that our ideas and opinions are largely influenced by self-interested, biased mediators of the news. As I illustrate later in this book, the news media shape the way we think about things, especially things that are foreign and frightening to us. Despite the fact that violent youth crime is a statistical rarity and that the victims are primarily other youth of the same social categories, the general populace perceives modern youth as increasingly violent and dangerous.

Three other features of the news media also warrant discussion. First, the Canadian newspaper industry is increasingly becoming monopolized by a few major media corporations. In effect, there is very little competition for the moral attention of Canadians (see Chapter 1 and Southern Ontario Newspaper Guild N.D.). Second, like most corporate entities, the "press" — at least at the decision-making/editorial level — is comprised of reporters, editors, producers, presenters and executive officers who are primarily white, male and privileged, and hence very much unlike the people who are the targets of their accounts. Third, the Canadian newspaper industry is highly competitive and is increasingly in competition with U.S. news organizations for the public's attention. More and more, the news media are also in competition with para-factual news accounts, which are based on real life events presented in a decontextualized, fictional style (for example, in television shows like *Cops* and *Dog, the Bounty Hunter*). Talk shows help erase the distinctions between fact and fiction by profiling individual cases as typical of larger social phenomena, as exemplified by Oprah Winfrey and especially Dr. Phil, who largely reduce discussions of social problems to individual choice and responsibility. The entertainment industry has invaded the news arena and obliterated the distinction between objectivity and subjectivity. For example, Don Cherry, the well-paid, controversial and very conservative commentator for the soap opera called *Hockey Night in Canada*, was inserted into CBC's coverage of the 2006 federal election, thereby trivializing and demeaning what is often seen as the bedrock of democracy — an election. It is clear that one of the singular characteristics of contemporary news reporting is that news is now, more than ever, a commodity that must be desirable and titillating if it is to sell.

It is important to note that the media may not just sell news, but sell audiences and programming to advertisers. As Hackett (1991) argues, advertisers are interested in two kinds of audience, the affluent and the mass audience. Newspapers and newsmagazines are prepared to pay more to reach affluent audiences because of their high purchasing power. Most importantly, however, "affluent readers are more likely to be politically conservative, and they have a disproportionate vote in determining the type and the political orientations of the media that survive" (Hackett 1991: 69). In addition, as the media become more monopolized, more concentrated and less competitive, the number of alternative voices and opinions diminishes, especially with respect to important political and social issues. This narrowing of opinion may reflect not necessarily consumer demand in general but the demands of particular consumers: advertisers and well-heeled audiences, who demand a particular world view or a particular take on social issues. This elitist world view is narrowly moral and necessarily alarmist.

The Consumer

The media's efforts to accentuate certain types of news is based on the presumption that what the public fears, the public will read about. I argue in this work that for reasons of marketing and competition, the media need to simplify the world for public consumption. Like fictional television, the news simplifies the world into binary opposites: good and evil, safe and frightening, and most importantly, us and them. The "mythical accounts" that they present become omnipresent truth which, through the democratic process, drives public policy. The obvious case in point is the law reform surrounding the *Youth Criminal Justice Act*, which has, at its core, a fundamental concern with public safety and dangerous youth.

The civil libertarian's response to biased news accounts is simply to let "the buyer beware." The suggestion is that if people do not like watching, reading or listening to partisan accounts of crime and deviance, then they have the freedom not to. Unfortunately, television is so much a part of ambient culture that the resolve not to listen is rarely possible; school-age children spend more time with the television than they do with their parents. As I alluded to earlier, with corporate concentration in the media, there are no, or very few, non-partisan accounts of crime or anything else. The choice becomes no choice — view the distortions or nothing at all! More importantly, as television continues to replace all other forms of media in the creation and transportation of news, the embracing nature of its influence becomes more alarming. It is the intrusive nature of television that is important in understanding why people cannot simply turn it off or tune it out:

> Television has achieved the status of meta-medium — an instrument that directs not only our knowledge of the world, but our knowledge of ways of knowing as well... television has achieved the status of "myth," as Roland Barthes uses the word. He means by myth a way of understanding the world that is not problematic, that we are nor fully conscious of, that seems, in a word, natural. A myth is a way of thinking so deeply embedded in our consciousness that it is invisible. This is the way of television.... Television has become, so to speak, the background radiation of the social and intellectual universe, the all-but-imperceptible residue of the electronic big bang of a century past, so familiar and so thoroughly integrated with American culture that we no longer hear its faint hissing in the background or see the flickering gray light. This, in turn, means that its epistemology goes largely unnoticed. And the peek-a-boo world it has constructed around us no longer seems even strange. (Postman 1985: 78–79)

While I disagree with Postman's contention that, "We are now a culture whose information, ideas and epistemology are given form by television, not by the printed word" (1984: 28), I argue that the print medium, in its need to appeal to the widest possible audience, has in fact adapted to the television world by becoming more like television in its fictional content and in its presentation of decontextualized, brief and episodic accounts. And, this pseudo-fact-based appeal to large audiences is what I believe is at the heart of accounts of youth crime and justice in Canada's print medium. Given the increasingly monopolistic trend in the Canadian newspaper and magazine industries, no longer can newspapers and magazines continue to appeal to a specific reading audience. The point is that the news media appeal to the prurient nature of the reading public (or more correctly, watching public), and the result is that the industry not only reacts to what the public wants but also proactively creates and directs the public appetite. A cursory look at a supermarket checkout stand is clear evidence that the worlds of fact and fiction are becoming more and more confused and fused, and that news stories are less verbal and more pictorial than in the past.

One of the ways that television has monopolized the attention of the public is by presenting very perfunctory versions of a large number of topics in a short period of time. To do this effectively, the medium uses pictorial images to bombard the viewer's senses with unconnected impressions. These impressions are of events that "do not arise out of historical conditions but rather explode from the heavens in a series of disasters that suggest a permanent state of crisis" (Postman 1988: 80). Increasingly, the different print media use visual images in disconnected contexts to emulate the visual effects of television. As I illustrate later in this book, magazines, especially, use stereotypical images that confront our emotions involving fear and security. These visual images are used, as well, by the newspaper industry, which employs stark headlines as surrogate pictures.

Ultimately, the audience for these theatrics is comprised partly of unwilling bystander consumers. I do not mean to suggest that people do not have volition: I mean only that news accounts that are presented in simplistic, consumable packages are so pervasive and so practical that the busy modern consumer cannot help but listen, if only subliminally. The news media, both factual and para-factual, have a great deal of influence on the modern mind, not necessarily because the people involved in the news are evil or manipulative, but rather because the market structure of the media industry dictates that the primary function of news reporting is that people pay attention.

Because the consumer, and not journalistic fidelity, is the focus of the news report, the mythical accounts of crime that pervade the news present a rather unmanageable world. The consumer is left with a sense of disjoint-edness, with a view of the world in which the human community does not work, and in which violence and personal trauma are ever-present realities. The news industry's presentation of the nihilistic society is no accident. Such presentations are constructed to sell and importantly, "they generate meaning as well as profit" (Hackett 1991: 51). The most insidious result of this manipulation is that the business of news acts as a "filter, gatekeeper, or agenda setter" (Hackett 1991: 52) that provides powerful citizens a mecha-nism to direct public opinion. As I argue in the pages to follow, this is exactly what has happened surrounding the mythology of youth crime in Canada.

Governments

One of the central principles of a critical approach to the study of crime and justice is that the control of crime is essentially a political act; it in-volves domination by wealthy men over poor men, by men over women, by politically dominant racial groups over marginalized racial minorities, and by enfranchised adults over children. If we take this as axiomatic, it is not difficult to see how issues of crime and punishment become politicized. As public fears are manipulated around issues of street crime and personal safety, the role of the politician and the centrality of public opinion in the democratic process come to the fore. Political platforms are, almost with-out exception, based on issues of crime and punishment. For the last three decades, right-wing political movements were fraught with arguments and images of a growing criminal underclass that increasingly preys on ordi-nary citizens. This fear and loathing is a natural playground for politicians. Criminality is pre-existent, it is cataclysmic and it demands severe and im-mediate intervention.

While some politicians understand that panics are exaggerated, they often choose to engage in the moral panic debates to appeal to the elector-ate. And, of course, no moral politician would oppose anything that pro-tects vulnerable citizens. On December 26, 2005, a fifteen-year-old girl was killed and six other people injured in a shoot-out in the Eaton's Centre in Toronto. The shooters were twenty and seventeen years old, and the dead and injured were innocent bystanders. Understandably, the nation was in shock over the lethalness of gunplay that is generally not typical of Can-ada. In response and in the midst of an election campaign, the leaders of all the political parties vowed to toughen Canada's justice system to deal with dangerous offenders, especially young offenders. Although the New Democratic Party (NDP) did discuss the need to deal with social inequal-ity and youth marginalization, it was virtually impossible for politicians to respond with anything but a "call to arms." Similarly, as we sympathize and empathize with the victims and their families, it is difficult for us to feel anything but anger and vengeance. Unfortunately, if politicians and policy brokers cannot maintain a balanced assessment of crime and punishment, the mindset of Canadians becomes one of vigilantism. The public's perception of crime and the reality of crime in Canada become disconnected, and those in positions of power and those who administer this power generally pick an easy target (in the case of the Toronto shooting, the residents of the Jane Finch area). Almost without exception, these targets are members of disaffiliated and disenfranchised communities. Government, in its quest to be responsive and effective necessarily takes sides against the marginalized. It is important to state here that as governments take a stand against the marginalized, they take the focus off issues of corporate and organized crime, which are more politically volatile and can even involve politicians and news barons themselves.

A second dimension of government that is important in understanding the mythologies of crime is that governments have the power and ability to contribute facts to the mythmaking mechanism. The Foucauldian perspective outlined in Chapter 2 addresses how knowledge brokers, especially those who have access to specialized information, can create and control a reality. A government database is a powerful source of information that is often used in attempts to understand anti-social behaviour. Government documents have legitimacy for several reasons: they are based on empirically gained information (the census and government surveys); they are public domain (only in an ideal sense, in that they are difficult to access, especially for the layperson); they are mystical unless the viewer understands quantitative social research methods; they are necessarily decontextualized; and consequently, they are often mediated by experts. It is at this point where expertise becomes impression management.

Many of the news reports that focus on youth crime invoke government-based information as infallible. Government crime statistics provide a sense of how much crime is occurring in a society and how rates have changed over time. The problem is that statistics are based on police or court records and not on actual crime committed; they are open to interpretation, and they offer no explanation or context for things that happen. As a result, crime rates are an indication of the workings of the justice system rather than the nature of criminality. They are also often an indication of how crime is defined and categorized — youth crime statistics are often presented as total crime rates, which group many types of crimes together. The moral panic surrounding youth is based on official total crime rates, arguing that youth crime is epidemic. The interpretable reality, however, is that much of current youth crime, much like the previous context of the *Young Offenders Act*, is based on violations of the provisions of the *Youth Criminal Justice Act* for rather harmless acts of vandalism and schoolyard antagonisms. To group these offences with those that create fear and panic is to exaggerate and distort the reality of youth misconduct quite severely.

Official crime rates are often also an indication of the political climate at any one point in time. A body of research has argued that official crime and imprisonment rates fluctuate primarily as a result of changes in socio-economic and political conditions and not as a result of increases in crime committed or increases in policing and incarceration (Schissel 1992; Cantor and Land 1985). Simply put, government policy, not criminals, creates crime rates.

The Policers

While the police are the front-line protectors of the society, they have a good deal of influence and discretion in producing images of criminality. In fairness to the police, they often respond to public and political demands. Their democratic mandate is not only to police reactively but to proactively intervene before crime occurs. The concept of proactive intervention or crime prevention is part of the current vernacular of community justice and social health and is considered by policy makers as a more effective, less expensive method of securing a safe society. But, in their struggle to discharge the community policing mandate, the police often take it upon themselves to focus on what they understand to be criminogenic neighbourhoods, generally in the inner city, where the police are more numerous, more visible and more assertive. This activity also fulfils a second function for the police: the existence, popularity and growth of the police is based on increasing the scope and intensity of law enforcement in marginalized neighbourhoods, often equated in the public's mind with dangerous neighbourhoods. In an ironic sense, a holistic, community-based approach to crime prevention may be contradictory to the popularity of large police forces.

In discussing the role of the police in moral panics, it is difficult to place blame or even responsibility. The police have a crime control mandate that is concordant with orthodox law-amd-order justice policies, but they are not trained to be peace officers. They are mandated politically and professionally to act swiftly and militarily. Part of this military-like aggressiveness has to do with how they perceive their own safety and their reputation as a police force. The police, as front-line workers, have vast credibility in the eyes of the public. When police officers act quickly and without reflection and self-analysis, their actions are potentially harmful for the targets of public panics. It may be police bureaucrats and not front-line officers who are

49

most responsible for fomenting panic. Police management is responsible for not only helping set and implement the crime control mandate — in lieu of the peace officer mandate — but police officials selectively represent crime accounts to public officials and the media by releasing particular sorts of information.

Moralizing Groups

Over forty years ago, Howard Becker (1963) coined the term "moral entrepreneur" to refer to those individuals who take a pro-active role in defining and controlling deviant behaviour. Moral entrepreneurs have a vested interest in seeing the moral movement come to fruition. They are crusaders who believe that an identifiable segment of the population is acting immorally and who have the influence, credibility and power to put their beliefs into the public arena. For Becker, moral entrepreneurs were either "rule creators," who operated from a self-righteous, elitist world view, and/or "rule enforcers," who operate from a more pragmatic, "job well done" world view but who often share the same value system as the rule creator.

At the time of Becker's publication, it was quite clear that many historical examples existed of individual entrepreneurs who were able to affect public policy. In Canada, for example, the influences of Mackenzie King and Emily Murphy on Canadian drug legislation (cf. Comack 1991 ; Green 1986) are noteworthy. In the United States, the influence of Harry Anslinger, the head of the Federal Bureau of Narcotics, who was instrumental in the creation of the *Marijuana Tax Act*, is typical of the 1930–1960 era in North America (cf. Becker 1963). Most importantly in these examples, however, is that individuals with political power were able almost single-handedly to initiate public policy on the basis of assumed dangerous groups or "folk devils." In both jurisdictions, the folk devils were ethnic minorities who were politically and democratically marginalized: Chinese immigrants in the case of Canada and Mexican immigrants in the case of United States.

Modern-day moral movements, unlike those in the past, are less directed by individuals and more directed by political/doctrinal groups that have a strong, vested economic interest in creating a stricter, more punitive and less forgiving society. As I will argue in the section on media tactics, many of the moral entrepreneurial groups are closely connected to orthodox political or religious groups. While public leaders often spearhead these groups, it is unlikely that these individuals have substantial influence. These groups tap into existent public fervour for their own political credibility and exacerbate the emotional levels of the debates.

A central question about reform groups seems to be whether they hold more sophisticated or at least more grounded understandings of social phenomena than do the media or political leaders. I would suggest that this probably is the case. Yet when media or political accounts of crime are infused with blame and danger, reform groups are intensely vulnerable to impression management. As Cohen (1980) argues, there is a potential towards overreaction and panic amongst the public. Why such groups tend to err on the side of right-wing, punitive politics, however, is a fundamental question that has to do with understanding the forces that create and control pubic discourse.

The Victim

In the criminal justice system, the victim is often forgotten when it comes time to decide on guilt or innocence, and especially in decisions regarding punishment. Victim welfare is rarely involved in judicial decisions. Ironically, when public panics arise over *supposed* increases in crime, the victim becomes the focus of concern. Many of the media representations discussed in Chapters 4 and 5 are presented from the point of view of the victim. Punishment-based political lobbies argue that they are protecting the innocent victim when they advocate harsher law-amd-order policies. And, of course, the victim's experience is a powerful political tool in that we all can imagine being the victim of a crime. It is relatively easy, therefore, for political persuaders to convince us to empathize with the plight of victims.

Victimization is used as a discursive mechanism in two ways. First, textual and pictorial depictions of victims' experiences are intended to evoke primal, passionate responses to fear of crime and potential victimization. The vicarious victim's experience frames our understanding of the criminal event and serves to create empathy not only for the victim but also for advocates of law and order. Second, explanations for youth deviance are made in the context of family and cultural victimization, and the insinuations include mother-centred and/or lower-class families as potentially predatory on their children.

We are left with these dual accounts of victimization, which establish that there is a need for panic and that innocent children are the victims of an uncaring, dangerous, poor class. Of course, victimization is a real problem that does impact on people's lives. We cannot refute or ignore that crime needs real solutions. However, the concept of victimization, as seen through a critical analytical lens, must be acknowledged as a volatile, powerful discursive tool that evokes collective passions and that feeds law-amd-order politics.

What is missing from popular cultural depictions of crime is a sense of larger victimization at the structural level, a sense of contextualization. What is important is how depictions are constituted in discourse that is, at

51

once, believable, instructive and policy-forming. There is a need to unpack the language of labelling, to identify the political and economic forces that drive the discourse and to analyze the political and economic advantages that accrue to the privileged from the denigration of marginalized, relatively powerless peoples.

Probably most importantly from a social justice point of view, crime panics and harsh law-amd-order programs miss or ignore a fundamental consideration in understanding crime: *most repeat young offenders and their families are victims of privation*. They are more than likely to be repeatedly victimized as clients of the systems of law, social welfare and education. These claims are categorically rejected by conservative political movements, which argue that people break the law for individualistic reasons and that in a free society, people have the freedom to choose between right and wrong. This immediately compelling and simplistic libertarian position is difficult to refute in a democratic society. I will show in Chapter VII, however, that for repeat young offenders, the background of victimization and privation presents a more compelling, more profound argument for understanding offenders than does the freedom of choice argument.

The Expert

Language and knowledge are social constructions and they have political power. They have the ability to define and explain "reality," to tell the "truth." People who foster and use moral panics have a vested interest in making their truth claims as valid and legitimate as possible — hence their use of experts: academics, doctors, pollsters and police and court officials. Such experts have access to specialized knowledge and specialized language that are both mystical and impressive. The credibility of many media and political accounts of crime is based on the "expert" testimony of relatively privileged people; professional testifiers are rarely drawn from the socio-economic strata that are occupied by stereotypical street criminals. We discredit common knowledge or folk wisdom and rely on the opinions of the educated. In contrast, community-based models of justice rely on the collective wisdom and advice of people from all places in the society.

It is important to note that professional knowledge is often uncertain and contradictory regarding the nature of crime and the use of punishment. Following Foucault, knowledge is essentially created and not discovered, and knowledge, in even the most "hard" sciences (like medicine and biology), changes depending on its political and historical context. As I illustrate in Chapters 4 and 5, representations of youth crime often draw on selected opinions that are not necessarily shared by the majority in a specific scientific community. The credibility of any expert statement is the result of the credentials of the author of the opinion and not based on the credibility of the account.

The Folk Devil

Finally, we come to the focus of the public panic. Cohen (1980) used the term folk devil to refer to those who are identified as threats to the moral and physical well-being of the society. The folk devil is identified by association with a particular, visible social category. Folk devils, as inherently deviant, are presumed to be self-seeking, out of control and capable of undermining the stability of the society. Importantly for the present work, folk devils are constructed in the context of moral panics, and they are imbued with stereotypical characteristics that set them apart from so-called normal, law-abiding society. This is why it is so easy for average citizens to become embroiled in the alarm over crime and to call for harsh justice. Most media depictions of crime, both factual and fictional, are about people unlike us, the street person, the drug trafficker, the violent and the amoral. Parenthetically, in the case of youth crime, and indeed for adult crime as well, this stereotype is largely inaccurate. In fact, most youth commit crimes at one time or another but their crimes are transitory and involve very little harm (Snyder and Sickmund 1995, Schissel 1993). I contend, however, that the creation of the folk devil as a type of "resident alien" is the primary reason why punishment-based lobbies are so successful. It is difficult to punish people who are like us or our children, but much easier to punish those we do not understand or with whom we do not empathize. The creation of folk devils is indeed xenophobia.

This study is about the politics of hatred and the politics of fear. At a very basic level, hatred and fear are political emotions that people in positions of political and economic power use to garner public opinion. Fear and hatred are staples of popular culture and, resultantly, of populist politics, and they are marked by their ambient and furtive nature. They exist as an unquestioned part of our ideology and our discourse, evidenced by the fact that hatred is fundamental to news accounts and fear is the vehicle for selling those accounts.

In *The Politics of Everyday Fear* (1993), Massumi argues that our social spaces have been saturated by fear and that fear is a basis for collective social experience. I would add that fear and hatred also contribute to a collective understanding of issues of right and wrong, which incidentally, have little to do with a universal or inherent morality. Fear and hatred are not abstractions and are not the result of power in a theoretical form. Instead, fear and hatred are the result of the actual imposition of the moral will by some over others. This imposition of will flourishes in public discourse, in which some speakers are more educated and consequently more influential than others.

The politics of fear and hatred, in the final analysis, is the mechanism through which we come to attach moral valuations to social categories. If we hate and fear someone or something, then it must be bad. I contend that the xenophobia that we feel collectively towards young people, when unpacked, reveals an ideological orientation that associates immorality with marginal social groups, identifiable by the defining categories of race, class and gender. The politics of fear and hatred is, in its basic form, the politics of stratification.

This book is an attempt to understand the mythical representations of young offenders (and indeed young people in general) that infuse the Canadian consciousness. The following chapters try to separate the reality from the fiction, and in so doing, locate the creation of the panic in a context of media, politics and ideological management.

CHAPTER 4

Blaming Children:
Media, Discourse and Representation

Reporting on youth crime not only sensationalizes it by focusing on the most brutal but rarest forms of youth misbehaviour (presenting the unusual as usual), it also decontextualizes almost all youth misbehaviour. Crime among young people is most often presented as being out of control, and the "causes" of their anti-social behaviour are seen to lie in youth themselves. There is hardly a media story that presents statistical trends or the kinds of youth crime with accuracy. Nor is there much connection between youth crime and the dispossessed position of youth in our society. For the past fifteen years, we have been inundated with images of young people who have no respect for anyone or anything and are simply out of control in a permissive society. Youth apprehension by the justice system, in reality, criminalizes being in a single-mother family, racial oppression and poverty. And, crime reporting blames the victims of inequality as those who directly or indirectly cause youth crime.

Since the mid-1990s, the form and content of the news reports about youth and young offenders have changed. Some of the reports are equally venomous over the whole time period, yet, in recent years many are more subtle, less directly offensive. The early 2000s focus on risk assessment, Fetal Alcohol Syndrome (FAS) and forensic science, for example, does not use the images and language of the gun-toting, snarling, violent youth of the early 1990s. At times, there appears to be some contextualization of the social position of young people, but the media still very powerful indicts young people as a culture and condemns the socially marginalized position of many young offenders.

Media Techniques and the Deconstruction of Crime

Reporting on youth crime, like much else in the media, shows the power of decontextualized accounts and the ability of the media messages to represent the unusual as usual. I wish to underscore that the primary function of these essentially ideological portraits of crime and criminals is to use selected, extraordinary, non-typical crimes as evidence of a general crime wave. These depictions of crime episodes receive little or no public censure, other than occasionally in academic literature. With respect to the format of crime accounts, it is important to notice the initial written and visual messages that appear. The first few paragraphs of a text and prominent pictures are very television-like in their perfunctory and cryptic approach to news. Postman argues that the

> news of the day is a figment of our technological imagination. It is quite precisely a media event. We attend to fragments of events from all over the world because we have multiple media whose forms are well suited to fragmented conversation. (Postman 1985: 8; see also Roberts and Foehr 2004; Fleras and Kunz 2001; Glassner 1999)

That the medium dictates the message is worth repeating here because it highlights a fundamental crisis confronted by the print medium: the ever-present ability of television to capture viewers' attention. And, I argue in this work, television does set the standards for viewer/reader likes and dislikes. Postman (1985) reiterates the importance of television in framing the modern ethic as

> the most significant American cultural fact of the second half of the twentieth century: the decline of the Age of Typography and the ascendancy of the Age of Television. This change-over has dramatically and irreversibly shifted the content and meaning of public discourse, since two media so vastly different cannot accommodate the same ideas. As the influence of the print wanes, the content of politics, religion, education, and anything else that comprises public business must change and be recast in terms that are most suitable to television. (1985: 8)

If attention to the written word is limited, as has been suggested for TV generation consumers (Postman 1985), the things encountered on initial perusal in newspaper and magazine articles are the ones that imprint on the minds of most readers. When this visual discourse (both pictorial and lingual) is studied carefully and critically, it becomes obvious that the messages are subtle, politically palatable and ideologically directed at and damaging to the image of youth. The depictions are not all the same, however, and the images can be categorized according to how they manage and manipulate the message. The message is the same, nonetheless, and it is simple: youth crime is endemic; it is unpredictable but characteristic of a certain kind of youth; and it requires dramatic and stern intervention. The remainder of this chapter illustrates the strategies — the categories of stories and the presentation techniques — that the news media employ to create a particular, partial view of youth crime that I argue is deliberately biased against all youth, but specifically against youth who occupy low socio-economic positions. Youth crime stories in all the print media fall into three main categories of decontextualization: the morality play, socio-economic blindness and expert opinion. As well, the media tend to frame these stories using a particular set of techniques: the presentation of the "facts" of crime, the reality of crime through pictures and the connection between evil youth and soft justice.

Youth Crime and the Morality Play

The first category of crime stories includes depictions of unusual youth crimes that appeal to people's sense of despair by concentrating on the horror, the potential for violent behaviour and bystander apathy. The accounts present youth crime as inexplicable and ultimately unthinkable. This type of depiction is a reverse morality play that appeals to our sense of righteousness and our fear of an amoral world. Most importantly, such accounts contain pervasive messages about the connections between morality and social position, and though they may attempt to be even-handed and objective, they lapse into social censure.

Just such a media account involves the case of James Bulger, a two-year-old British child who was abducted by two boys under the age of thirteen in a Liverpool shopping centre; he was dragged away along a railway track and beaten to death. This incident happened in plain view of passersby who failed to help, for reasons speculated on at great length by the media.

This case is noteworthy in part for the horrific nature of the crime and young age of the convicted, but it is most noteworthy in its evolution into a morality play. As Bradley (1994) argues, "this rarest of murders has been transformed into a symbol of everything that is wrong with Britain today" (12). (For more recent analyses of the case, see Alison Young 1996 and Richard Collier 1998.) The search for a rational explanation for the murders, which was the original media focus, was replaced by a protracted campaign to understand this crime as the result of the worst side of the human condition. The argument that evil incarnate is part of the human condition forewarns the potential in all citizens to become like the murderers of James Bulger. For, if ten year olds, who in our estimation are too young to have had the chance to become corrupted, are capable of this behaviour, then so are we all.

The class-based nature of this account became evident when newspapers such as *The Sun* and the *Evening Standard* began speculating about the potential of certain kinds of families to persist outside of civilized society.

State institutions (including the justice system and social services), along with conservative politicians and investigative reporters, engaged in class-oriented rhetoric surrounding the competency of parents in raising moral children. All three sources of opinion began to discuss the parents of the accused as somehow part of the flawed underclass, with typical pejorative attributes such a single motherhood and broken homes. The discourse centred on the classic cases of abuse and neglect that were deemed to be the result of privation; by extension, all children living in privation or in broken homes were at risk. This reactionary backlash harkens back to the turn-of-the-century justice system, which was preoccupied with detecting pre-delinquency on the bases of social and cultural behaviour.

As Bradley (1994) points out, the resulting political debates about the Bulger murder called for more moral intervention and classical punishment and attacked liberal politics. The drama that was played out after the crime portrayed nihilistic criminal behaviour as being the result of the drift into immorality by the lower classes (with the attendant criminogens of pornography, alcohol and promiscuity). Liberal social policies were blamed.

By fictionalizing and exploiting the tragedy of the victim, the media, in concert with conservative politicians, were able to nurture a public panic that resulted in the call for more law and order and more intervention into the lives of marginalized families. Most noteworthy in this type of crime depiction is its ability to reconstruct and recontextualize the events of one case into a societal framework in which moral breakdown, class privation and the devolution of family values are indicted. The oppressive potential of a highly classed society and the immorality of blaming and punishing the victim of economic forces are disregarded. The mechanism of this disregard is illustrated in the second strategy for producing crime accounts.

Socio-Economic Blindness

A second category of depictions illustrates how media reporting tends to remove crime from its socio-economic context and recast it in moralistic and emotional frames of reference. The first example is noteworthy in its blatant disregard for objectivity, its calculated attempt to create despair with the use of exaggeration and visually horrific images, and most importantly, in describing the events of a horrific youth crime in a business-like manner. The visual image in this depiction in the *Montreal Gazette* is obviously intended to represent youth in a particularly lethal context and provokes a visceral aversion to the young antagonist. The dark image is one of a competent young gunman, brandishing a weapon in an obvious show of bravado. The first narrative we encounter is that of an incomprehensible act of youth violence. Several short paragraphs explain the crime in a detached police-style report, followed by unequivocal pronouncements that childhood crime is worse now than at any other time in Canadian history, a statement that is not only untrue but unsubstantiated (see Chapter 6). Any sense that there are other reasons for kids committing crimes is left to the last few paragraphs of a rather lengthy article. The more even-handed discussions relating social inequality and lack of support services for marginalized kids is relegated to a truncated discussion at the end; the ideological potency of this article appears well before this.

This type of depiction removes the offence and the offender almost entirely from the socio-economic and legal context in which crimes occur. The producers of the message implicitly suggest that crime is a matter of inherent evil, that it is manifested in defiant, gun-wielding behaviour. By using alarmist untruths — "But the 12 to 17 year-old set is killing, raping, and assaulting more than ever before" (*Montreal Gazette* 1989: B1) — the article creates, at the outset, a framework for reading the rest of the article.

The next article, although much shorter and even-handed, once again reads like a police report, supplemented with speculations about crime and youth violence. In Chicago in September of 1994, an eleven-year-old boy was murdered in a gangland type slaying. The article in the news services (*Saskatoon Star Phoenix*, August 31, 1994: D12) concentrated on the child's affiliations with gang members, the types of crimes he had committed in his young career (including the gang-related murder of a fourteen-year-old girl), and the lamentations of community leaders who blamed the system for failing the child. The article then changes abruptly to discuss an investigation by social services that revealed that the boy had been scarred by systematic physical abuse in his family and that social services had intervened unsuccessfully. The article focuses on him being taken from his mother and placed in the care of his grandmother, who eventually relinquished custody to welfare agencies. The final words in the article, supplied by a local police superintendent, are a message to all youth that the promises of gangs often have fatal consequences.

In summary, the article evokes sympathy for the child offender/victim and laments the inability of the system to effectively care for the child. But mostly, the article concentrates on the family's pathology, the suggestions of a broken home headed by women and the implications that gangs are at the core of the criminal world. While half-truths are present in the article, the major misrepresentation occurs through omission. The article ignores the socio-economic context in which the child and his family dwell, the economic reality of social welfare agencies that are financially unable to carry out their mandates, and the reality of industrialized societies that discard people to make a profit. What is missing in the journalistic analyses, besides

Figure 4.1 Saskatoon Star Phoenix, August 31, 1994:D12

Murder suspect found in pool of blood

Chicago (AP)—His nickname was Yummy. In a short life filled with abuse, he was prosecuted at least eight times for robberies and other crimes before police suspected him of shooting one teenager dead and wounding two others.

Police started hunting for Robert Sandifur. They found him Thursday in a pool of blood beneath a railway overpass. He was 11.

His body—not yet five feet, not quite 70 pounds—lay about seven blocks from where police believe he opened fire Sunday at two different groups of boys, killing a 14-year-old girl, Shavon Dean, about 10 metres from her home.

Robert was suspected of having gang ties. Two gunshot wounds—one to the back of the head, one to the top—led police to suggest fellow gang members had killed him. Authorities had a suspect in the boy's slaying.

Solemn neighbors gathered around the pool of Robert's blood in the South Side neighborhood of neat yards and well-kept homes. Adults showed young children the wet blood as a warning.

"This is our problem," Valerie Jordan said. "The authorities and the system have failed. This is our child. The young lady that was killed, that was our baby."

In the last two years, Robert was prosecuted for robbery, car theft, arson and burglary. He was convicted twice and received probation, although one judge sentenced him to three weeks of detention for probation violations.

Robert was no stranger to the state's child welfare agency, either.

A 1986 investigation by the Department of Children and Family Services found scars on Robert's face, cordlike marks on his abdomen and leg, and cigarette burns on his buttocks.

Robert was taken from his mother and placed with his grandmother, who nicknamed him Yummy for his love of cookies. Complaints that she was not supervising the boy led to his placement in a juvenile facility in 1993, but he ran away.

In July, a judge returned Robert to his grandmother until the boy could be put in an out-of-state detention centre that permits children to be locked in or physically restrained, both of which are forbidden in Illinois.

Robert's grandmother, Janie Fields, became hysterical before she shut the door on reporters.

"I really can't say what I'm going through," she said. "but I know my baby's not here anymore and I can't say I love you Robert anymore."

Police Supt. Matt Rodriguez said the boy's death should send a message to other youths that "the promises of the gangs . . . are not promises of things that are good."

Reprinted with express permission of Associated Press.

the context of the crime, is the reality of this child as a survivor. It is remarkable in one sense that an eleven-year-old child can survive on the streets on his own for three years. When legitimate avenues of support fail, it is understandable that the only context for such survival is gang affiliations. His struggle to survive is neither pathological nor indicative of a degenerating society. It is more likely, in fact, a normal human response.

The most striking sentiment expressed in both articles is that these deaths and the crimes that precipitated them are indicative of a generation of children out of control. The articles leave the reader with a sense of foreboding that nothing is to be done and that stricter crime control measures, while not solutions, are the only possible reactions. The reader is left with reason for panic. Apparently nihilistic behaviour at such a young age is an affront to our collective desire to care for the young, for when the young are corrupted, the society must be morally self-destructive. The sense of pessimism inherent in such accounts is a powerful indictment that nothing is working and that something corrective must be put into place. The insinuations are that the problems of youth are individual, family-based problems that need interventionist, punitive solutions rather than socio-economic support.

A third example illustrates how public discourse is blind to the class-based nature of society. The ideology of blaming individuals and their families, coupled with the need for judicial intervention, is bolstered by "medical" discourse, which, in turn, masks the reality that many of the problems that individuals suffer have their origins in social inequality. However, the genetic theme of congenital illness presents a compelling story that allows experts to focus in on the individual and "find" the root cause of crime, exemplified by a "syndrome." As I argue in Chapter 5, fetal alcohol syndrome (FAS), fetal alcohol effect (FAE) and fetal alcohol spectrum disorder (FASD) clearly have a biological reality, but it is important to consider that when we create a language that associates crime with medical abnormality, we eliminate other ways of looking at crime. Or, in a more insidious way, we relate sickness, such as cognitive damage, to maternity, motherhood, child-rearing and social class and end up condemning the poor and the racialized as less moral than white, relatively wealthy citizens. In public discourse about morality, mother-blaming, race-blaming and class-blaming predominate in some not so subtle ways.

In March 2004, the Victoria *Times-Colonist* ran an article on FAS/FAE, suggesting that, "It's not as if the effects of fetal alcohol exposure are newly discovered. Even in the Old Testament (Judges, chapter 13), an angel warns a pregnant women to drink no wine or strong drink" (Watts 2004: D1). The *Globe and Mail* ran a similar report in February 2003 entitled, "Middle class

FAS: A silent epidemic." The report defines the "epidemic" and then suggests that the racial dimension, that FAS/FAE is an Aboriginal phenomenon, misses the "fact" that "The lion's share of federal funding for FAS is poured into programs exclusively for native children, a richly deserving population, but hardly alone" (Philp 2003: 1). A more blatant example of both race-blaming and mother-blaming occurred in *The Report Newsmagazine* in April 2001. The article is interesting and disturbing in that it uses provocative, discriminatory language that seems out of place in twenty-first-century journalism, but because it is framed within the context of medical research carried out in Inuvik, NWT, by a major university, the vicious language tends to be supported by medical discourse. The article states, "Of the school's children in Grades 1 to 3, 40% of Inuit and one-third of Indians had mothers who had binged while carrying them, according to a recent study by four University of Alberta paediatricians…. None of the Caucasians in those grades had mothers who binged" (cited in White 2001: 1).

The casting of blame subverts the more important reality of children and health, that poverty and poor nutrition predispose children to extreme jeopardy. These are not individual, familial or cultural shortcomings; they are the shortcomings of the socio-economic system. In fact, Bingol et al. (1987) showed quite clearly that the rate of FAS among children of low-income women was 71 percent compared to 4.5 percent for higher-income women, *despite levels of alcohol use*. The study revealed the key difference between the two groups to be nutrition. Such work, although not definitive, tells us legions about the nature of how we condemn the dispossessed. Such findings also show how medicine, despite its philanthropic mandate, is part of the rhetoric of condemning children and youth (and their families) for their imputed failings. The fetal alcohol discourse is built, at least in part, on scientific uncertainty, moral panics, and our fundamental belief in the immorality of poverty.

This last article provides an apt transition into the next section, which illustrates how truth claims by public commentators are reinforced and given credibility by invoking science and the discourse of "experts."

Truth and the Discourse of Experts

The following example illustrates how crime is decontextualized in media discourse by drawing on the panic of pathology and endorsing it with the expert opinion. The article is taken from a 1994 issue of *Maclean's* magazine, the cover story of which is entitled, "Kids Who Kill, Special Report." The cover page shows a young man dressed in jeans, t-shirt and an inverted ball cap holding a gun in a fashion that depicts his ability and familiarity with the weapon. Most striking about the pictorial depiction is the ordinary and typical dress of the lethal youth.

The article discusses three Canadian cases in which young offenders committed murder. The individual cases are presented in temporal and graphic detail and are accompanied by family photographs of the victims and their relatives, a grisly crime scene and one of the young offenders in a prison garden. The articles concentrate on several dimensions of teenage criminality and imply that these levels of explanation are the most rational and fundamental and, consequently, offer the most hope for the control of deadly violence amongst youth. The first suggestion is that youth crime is erratic and unpredictable and by implication, is threatening to everyone. The article invokes expert medical testimony to attest to the psychotic and inherent natures of these acts; youths like these — and the article stresses the ordinariness of their communities and activities — can be everywhere; these psychopathic killers are housed in the bodies of normal appearing youth. The reader is left with the impression that a youth killer (and youth criminals in general) could be the boy — and about that the article is extremely gendered — next door.

The second suggestion that we see in the profiles of the three murders is part of the attempt to unpack and reconstruct the psychic lives of the young killers. The report focuses on elements of outside influence such as exposure to pornography, the emulation of notorious movie criminals (the movie *Silence of the Lambs* is mentioned several time throughout the article), and the dysfunctionalities of family styles, including strict discipline, lax discipline, absentee fathers, single motherhood and poverty. The ostensible markers of delinquency are introduced into the criminality equation as warning signs for pathological behaviour.

The preamble to the three case studies is quite telling in its representation of the "problem of youth crime." The language is laden with sinister references to the unique predatory nature of the young killer. The introduction offers a litany of inexplicable killings by children that at the time raised the public pressure to reform the *Young Offenders Act*. The last paragraph in the article, however, hypothesizes that what youth criminals have in common is a "stunning lack of empathy" for their victims. The article finally calls on the work of an eminent psychiatrist to make sense of the youth crime wave; his conclusion is that more adolescents are now borderline psycho- and socio-pathic personality types, "like the characters in the *Silence of the Lambs*" (*Macleans* 1994: 33), than in the past. The psychiatrist's last warning is to the irresponsible parent for creating young people like Hannibal Lechter, the brutal psycho-pathic killer in the movie. While the article attempts to be even-handed in explaining the position of detractors, who argue for the lenient handling of young offenders, the journalistic slant is

Figure 4.2 Maclean's, August 15, 1994, cover

Kids Who Kill
Special Report: Why three young Canadians committed murder

Reprinted with express permission of MacLean's Magazine.

that, somehow, the youth generation is nihilistic and that state social control mechanisms are not doing enough to curb the increasing youth violence in our society.

The overall article does present a compelling case for the continual attempt to understand and deal with youth killers. It would be impossible for anyone not to feel and share the extreme tragedy and loss felt by the victims and their relatives and communities. And, of course, there is a continuing need to protect people from harm. What the article transmits, however, is a sense of helplessness in the face of increasing homicide by youth (a belief that is empirically unsupported, see Chapter 6) that are characteristic of a degenerating youth culture. By invoking experts and their discourse, the article presents youth violence as unexceptional and commonplace, and by speculating on the origins of youth criminality, this type of discourse recirculates moral indictments against family types, social classes and gendered environments. What we are left with is a constructed world that is polarized into good and bad, where criminals are of a certain social caste, a world in which the answers to problems, once again, are to be found in law and order and in the "wisdom" of forensic science and medicine.

Another article based on the theme of forensic understanding of youth crime illustrates how blatant forms of the discourse are relatively easy to decipher. In February 2004, *The Vancouver Sun* carried an article entitled, "Armed teens do more crimes, study finds" (Feb 3, 2004: A10). The thrust of the article was that scientists had determined that teens with conduct disorder are more likely to carry guns than those without and that older teens are more likely to carry guns than younger teens. The entire article is curiously simple in its logic and very damning in its implication that teens are the problem. Guns are not the problem. Medical conditions — conduct disorder — are the danger. The article cites research that suggests that mothers may also be responsible for the problem: "disturbed boys whose parents let them run wild are more likely to commit crimes than those with parents who keep them under better supervision. 'Maternal psychopathy' — psychiatric trouble diagnosed in mothers of these boys — doesn't do them a world of good either" (*The Vancouver Sun*, Feb 3, 2004: A10). For the reader of this article the research is supposed to be obvious. The sarcasm and the telling of the research story are indicative, once again, of a medicalized discourse that is irrefutable in the eyes of the public.

Scientific Research, Empirical
Evidence and the "Facts" of Crime

A current reality in news reports of young offenders involves the importance of science and research in understanding young people's delinquency. The stories that are framed in this paradigm of empiricism and research are often neglectfully biased and hateful. The following examples illustrate this phenomenon. In many respects, articles that deal with youth crime and race can become very racist in their quest for scientific evidence about evil youth. An article in *The Vancouver Sun*, May 4, 2004, entitled. "Federal study: Blame parents for soaring Indo-Canadian youth crime," relates the results of a federal study of Indo-Canadian crime in the Vancouver area funded by Heritage Canada. The article uses the clever device of relying on verbatim statements by Indo-Canadian girls, boys, single mothers, social workers and male community leaders to make the point that

> Brutal criminal violence by Indo-Canadian male youths over the past decade is being blamed on a culture clash that has driven deep divisions between children and their parents.... Immigrants from India are in many cases too focused on making a living to help guide their children. (A1, reprinted with express permission of the Vancouver Sun.)

The statements, based on focus group discussions, are lumped together to produce an "evidenced based" report that directly blames the cultural parenting practices of Indian immigrants to Canada for the "epidemic" of youth violence in Vancouver. Sample statements include:

> Families have abandoned their children. They came from India to get rich, but nobody sees their kids any more, and they are getting away from religion. (community leader)

> When kids hear their father curse at their wives and the wives take it, how can it not affect our kids? (single mother)

> Our community tends to cover things up. This contributes to the problem. (social worker)

> Sometimes parents expect boys to fight and even encourage it. They get embarrassed if their kids do not fight and hold their own. (young woman)

The most damning statements in the report are left to justice officials outside of the Indo-Canadian community. These comments are interspersed within the comments by Indo-Canadian interviewees as if there is cross-cultural consensus about the problem:

> The young Indo-Canadian males that come to our attention are dreadfully spoiled and pandered to.... The family denies there is a problem and consider[s] their sons to be princes. (crown prosecutor)

> The lack of hierarchy in the crime groups, and the extreme level of violence among Indo-Canadians... is not characteristic of more sophisticated biker and Asian gangs in the Lower Mainland, who see high profile violence as 'bad for business.' (Organized Crime Agency of BC)

> Violent crime is strongly influenced by the culture of this current generation of Indo-Canadian youth.... There appears to be a consistent pattern where Indo-Canadian criminals are from families who provided their sons with money, freedom, favouritism and a discipline inconsistent with their siblings (primarily female), coupled with the culture's distrust of the police and an emphasis on preserving the face or honour. (police official).

This *Vancouver Sun* article is interesting in several regards. First, blatant racism gets lost among out-of-context statements by a litany of insiders and outsiders in the Indo-Canadian community. Second, the discourse of cultural blame gets mixed with family blame. Orthodox criminology often explores issues of family and culture to understand delinquency. Family issues are used here to legitimate the arguments regarding race and culture; the basic sentiment is that families still lie at the heart of young people's immorality, even if family practices are largely cultural practices. Third, when we strip away the talk about crime, the characteristics of "criminogenic" families described in the article are characteristics that could be applied to any middle-class family in any context: families provide their kids with money and freedom; parents work hard to provide for their families, often not being able to spend as much time as they would like with their kids; families are focused on making a living; newcomers mistrust the police; boys are encouraged to hold their own in confrontations; parents fight. However, when the litany of comments and family/cultural characteristics are strung together, the result is a convincing report that indicts Indo-Canadian people in general for waves of violence. Shockingly, the report, from which the article draws its information, is lent credibility by its funding through Heritage Canada, a public organization whose mandate is to promote racial harmony. Like many of the modern journalistic devices described in this book, this report amasses "evidence" and in a pseudo-scientific way, produces facts, many of them from the targets of the report, that prove the point. In the science of forensics, hard facts are less necessary than opinions by experts and insiders. As I have discussed in a previous section, the role of the expert is solidified when hard science frames the debates.

Another way that media accounts invoke the importance of empiricism is to produce a litany of hard evidence, much like in a court of law. The examples here are taken from several years ago, and while this technique although still in vogue, is less common than the technique described above, in which science-based research becomes the source of facts. Nonetheless, the listing of "facts" is often used to portray the darkest side of youth crime, as police-based evidence that teen violence is on the rise. *The Vancouver Sun*, (September 19, 1992: A1), for example, contained an extremely large byline accompanied by a box entitled, "A Year of Youth Mayhem," listing seven youth crimes presented in official, police-report format. *Western Report* (May 4, 1992: 19–20), in the same year, used the headline, "Youth Crime and Coddling," accompanied by a picture of five youths walking in a mall in Edmonton. Under the picture is the subtitle "mall prowling." Besides the presentation of teens walking in a mall as prowling, most important in this article is the large boxed-off section entitled, "Typical Teenage Terror," which lists teen crimes occurring in the Edmonton area. This litany of crimes is interesting in that severe depictions are interspersed with less severe acts of teenage deviance; this creates images that are both unethical and appear to be only for the purposes of fear-mongering.

That these defiant and deviant acts are criminal is not in question here. What is suspect is the imputation that they are all acts of terror and are typical teenage crimes. The message is reinforced by the picture of typical young male youths "prowling" in a mall, versus simply "hanging out." Interestingly, of the ten crimes that are listed as teenage terror, four involve vehicle theft, a debatable categorization as a terrifying crime. Official crime statistics show quite clearly that the majority of crimes for which teens were arrested and charged at this time were for breaches of the *Young Offenders Act* and defiance of the courts, minor acts of theft and vandalism, drug violations and minor assaults (cf Chapter 7; Bell 2002; Alvi 2000; Schissel 1995a; Winterdyk 1995).

The final example of evidence-based reporting uses the same technique of bombarding the reader with a recital of crime, but employs a somewhat different presentation to produce the same effect. The article entitled, "A generation of outlaws: Wildly rising teen crime is blamed on a molly-coddle law" (*Western Report*, Feb. 24, 1991: 18) begins with two depictions of teen crimes, one involving the robbery of a convenience store and one involving vandalism and automobile theft. What is striking about the presentations is the inclusion of the victim's wishes and fears and testimonials by police that the kids involved are completely out of control and unrepentant. The audience is essentially attuned to the forthcoming "facts."

The list of crimes is presented after the sensationalized depictions have created an atmosphere of alarm and anger in the audience. In this instance, the list involves a series of official statistics for the province of Alberta that are contextualized in a discussion of increasing crime rates and an increasing number of chronic offenders. The focus of the "facts" are once again vehicle thefts, total crimes (without an explanation that most of these crimes are minor), and attendant commentary on the habitual nature of youth crime.

This last example is taken from a *Vancouver Sun* report from June 10, 2005, entitled, "A history of organized crime in the Indo-Canadian community." I said at the outset of this section that the news reporting technique of bombarding the audience with a litany of crimes was less common now than a few years ago, but the following blatant example shows clearly that the technique is still part of a newspaper repertoire of alarmist journalism. The report presents a chronicle of about forty murders involving Indo-Canadian men in Vancouver over an eight-year period as evidence of an epidemic of violence. Each description contains the names of the victims, their ages, the name of the offender (if available) and considerable discourse about Indo-Canadian gangs and organized crime. By isolating only murders involving Indo-Canadian men and by identifying them by name, the article deliberately restricts the panic over organized violence to Indo-Canadian people. By presenting the murders that occurred over an eight-year period in a concise package, readers are confronted by a group of crimes that, when lumped together, certainly evoke a sense that there is a reign of terror in Vancouver that is linked to the Indo-Canadian community, when over that period of time the crimes are quite uncommon. By presenting the ages of the victims and offenders — almost all in their teens or early twenties — the article, as with the others in this section — focus violent crime on the young. And by presenting the crimes like a police incident report, the article draws on forensic facts for its credibility. This article and the two previous examples collapse police-like reports of crimes over time into a cross-sectional frame that appears to the reader as an epidemic. In this way, the reports create alarm and panic and deliberately focus that alarm on an identifiable segment of the Canadian population, branding the entire culture as dangerous.

The techniques of presenting a listing of crimes and crime statistics and the use of empirical evidence based on research are significant for several reasons. First, they force the reader into viewing crimes that take place over a lengthy period in one visual frame, creating an illusion of a crime wave. Second, the empiricism is compelling in that it is not far removed from objective, empirical journalistic style except for some of the editorializing language — and it is very much in the vein of law, which uses evidence as the cornerstone of "truth and justice. What the reader is left with is a snapshot of an official crime wave.

The Picture as Reality:
The Power of Pictorial and Verbal Snapshots

Stark headlines and sensational photos are the stock in trade for the news media. Both are designed to capture the reader's attention and to frame the discussions in a predetermined ideological context. Television uses the technique of flash images and brief, out-of-context images to attract and capture the attention of the viewer (Roberts and Foehr 2004; Leishman and Mason 2003; Postman 1994). The attraction of news on television is that it simplifies and condenses the news into something immediately understandable and yet immediately foreign and aversive. Pictures have a "primordial power." News on television is like a never-ending series of first impressions, and the impact of first impressions cannot be overstated in news reports. This is exemplified by the articles that follow.

A very stark example is the cover story for the July 31, 1995, edition of *Alberta Report*. The pictorial images are blatant and unapologetic. The image is one of a criminal-looking girl adorned with several earrings, brandishing a weapon and with an obvious inclination to shoot. And, of course, the first sentiment we see is that feminism and the liberation of women are directly responsible for a boom in violence by girls. On the next page, we see a brief abstract of the cover story retitled, "Killer Girls." It is here where journalistic licence seems to be supplanted by abject bias and journalistic distortion.

The brief description asserts that the "recent crop" of teenage girls — all teenage girls by implication — can be as "malicious" and "evil" as boys (again all boys by implication). Further, the synopsis declares an explosion in youth crime, against an abundance of evidence to the contrary. And, finally, feminism and the struggle for gender equality are indicted as criminogenic.

The first page of the article contains a picture of the gun-wielding girl

Figure 4.3 Alberta Report, July 1995, cover

Reprinted with express permission of United Western Communication.

Figure 4.4 Alberta Report, July 31, 1995:1

Killer girls

Girls, it used to be said, were made of sugar and spice. Not anymore. The latest crop of teenage girls can be as violent, malicious and downright evil as the boys. In fact, they're leading the explosion in youth crime. It's an unexpected byproduct of the feminist push for equality.

Reprinted with express permission of United Western Communication.

from the front cover with a headline that reads, "You've come a long way, baby: Prodded by feminism, today's teenaged girls embrace anti-social male behaviour." Once again, the messages are clear and repetitive. The reader, searching for the cover article, is besieged with a series of deliberate images and messages that frame the discussion in a framework of loathing that, as I will argue later, borders on hate literature.

A *Chatelaine* (May 1993) article is much more subtle, but it similarly uses visual emphasis to highlight and frame its vitriolic argument. The article on youth crime and justice is based on the premise that youth are an identifiable subculture that evolving into a counterculture in defiance of adult society. The first page of the article, however, is framed with a rather glaring sentiment that, in large letters, occupies one-third of the page:

> Violent-crime charges against kids have more than doubled in five years. Does this mean we are raising a generation of weapon-bearing, head-smashing monsters? An encounter with one young felon leads Patricia Pearson to explore the dark side of teen culture. (1993: 74)

This opening is obviously intended to be grab attention. On the next page we see another statement set off in large letters in the middle of the text which reads, "Teenagers like intimidating people. They like the power, it makes them feel good" (1993: 75). For the viewer who casually glances through the magazine, these statements are impossible to miss, and while the text may be more even-handed in its understanding of the problem of youth crime, the implications of the visual stimuli are clear and pointed. By presenting a rhetorical question in graphic and value-laden language — "weapon bearing, head-smashing monsters" — the reader is left with the impression that the possibility exists that the *entire* generation is headed in a terrifying direction. Further, the article suggests that violent-crime charges have more than doubled in five years without commenting on the changes in the practice of justice and policing that may have prompted such increases. These decontextualized statements appear as truths. A thorough reading of the article does show that these sentiments are qualified and contextualized somewhat. But, the problem remains that the first impression is very damning of youth.

The second statement again reads like an axiomatic truth about teenagers. As we find in the text of the article, this is a statement made by one police officer in Ottawa as he speculates on why teenagers engage in violence. Aside from the subjective nature of this comment, the out-of-context use of the statement in large, bold print creates an ideological frame for reading the article — if the entire article is indeed read by most people. The cursory reader sees only this "visceral truth" — that teenagers in general are intimidating and power hungry. This is an alarmist statement about the human condition.

Like television images on the evening news, the two stark verbal images on the first two pages of the article are intended for quick consumption. Like television as well, the statements are unambiguous in their indictment of youth, presented as a clear, bifurcated and ultimately consumable sentiment.

Evil Youth and "Soft" Justice

One of the most obvious and blatant techniques by which the media build an image of offensive youth is through declarations, often endorsed by professional experts, that children are inherently evil and that youth misconduct is the result of uncontrolled natural impulses. The ideological message is that these inherently vile beings need strict family discipline, or failing that, they require institutional intervention. Most of the depictions of horrific crimes are framed in this type of "nature versus nurture" discourse, in which nature seems to win out and in which "tough law and order" is an absolute necessity.

The following two examples illustrate the type of rhetoric surrounding the evil nature of youth that I included in *Blaming Children*. I follow these two examples from several years ago with an example of how current discourse — somewhat more subtle in its condemnatory talk — implicates law reform and "liberal" society for unleashing dangerous youth onto society. In all of these accounts, the technique of portraying youth as naturally evil is quite explicit.

Chatelaine magazine (May 1993 66(3): 75, 76) used just such a technique: in addition to the condemnatory headlines addressing the "Dark Side of Teen Culture," the article offers that teenagers, as a generic group "like intimidating people" (75). The article, somewhat less blatant in its attack on the nature of youth than the headline, discusses some of the reasons that youth engage in anti-social behaviour, but returns frequently to a generic teen culture that is "outlaw" and collectively defiant of the "accepted rituals of the society" (76). Finally, the article declares that because of society's inability to isolate the primary cause of teenage misconduct, "isolating each cause is not better than describing individual parts of an elephant — you don't account for the nature of the beast." "Nature" and "beast" references leave little doubt in the reader's mind that biology produces the evil human animal; this didactic position is visually reinforced with large, alarmist headlines.

A second example of inflammatory attacks on youth uses a cover page with the picture of a child in handcuffs, showing the child from the neck down. The cover story, entitled "Junior Gone Wild: An Aging Do-Your-Own-Thing Generation Lashes Out at its Savage Offspring" (*Alberta Report*, May 9, 1994) is followed by the lead article entitled, "Locking Up The Wild Generation" (again in large, dark type). The article is typical of many such diatribes against youth in its presentation of a litany of alarming violent crimes perpetrated by youth and in its professed frustration with being unable to explain such behaviour. Like most doctrinal attacks on youth, the visual/verbal referents are to a generic youth culture and its savage nature.

In their current form, such condemnatory articles are somewhat more subtle although the sentiment that remains is that kids are still inherently bad. The talk now, though, has turned to the youth justice system, which is held largely responsible because of its leniency. However, the news accounts are still rife with views that youth are as bad as or worse than before and that the courts cannot handle the epidemic of youth crime (in contrast to the actual crime trends, which do not bear this out). In 2005, the *National Post* published an article on young offenders entitled, "58 arrested in crime blitz" (April 19, 2005: A10). The newspaper describes what it calls a "blitz" — a ten-day program whereby York regional police focused on youth crime, especially youth designated as high risk offenders, in a raid than involved over a hundred arrests, the majority of which were for failing to comply with and breach of probation. The report was, in fact, a chronicle of a rather benign crime raid, which did not warrant the sensationalist *National Post* headline.

Another *National Post* report, entitled, "Some youth crimes deserve time," blamed the *Youth Criminal Justice Act* for not providing courts with the power to lock-up young persons who may be dangerous. The argument is based on a story in which five teenagers placed shards of glass in a Burlington playground, were caught and were sentenced to thirty days' house arrest and a hundred hours of community service. The report is emphatic in its condemnation of the justice system:

> Residents living near the playground, and especially parents of young children who were put at risk by the malicious stunt, have every reason to be outraged by the leniency of the sentence. Canadians across the nation should be concerned, too, because the teenagers' sentence is not an anomaly or the idiosyncratic result of an indulgent judge's soft spot for rebellious youth. Rather, it is the inevitable consequence of the country's two-year old Youth Criminal Justice Act (YCJA) which bends over backwards to prevent

young offenders from being sentenced to custody.... Because of the danger it caused, the booby-trapping of the Burlington playground was such an action. The only way to signal the seriousness of the life-threatening mischief, both to the offenders and those who might be tempted to do something similar, would have been to sentence the guilty teenagers to time in detention. But the YCJA effectively removes that option from a judge's list of choices.

Consequently, young people will soon learn, if they have not already, that breaking the law and endangering the well-being of others exacts little cost.

We are not doing anyone a service by fostering an environment of permissiveness: not to the young people who will be deprived of strong moral authority that would otherwise serve as an incentive to stay on the straight and narrow path; and not to the other members of society who will become their victims. Canada cannot afford to embrace the ideal of rehabilitation to the exclusion of the realistic necessity of punishment. If we continue to do so, we fill find ourselves facing a generation of young offenders who are bolder, more defiant and less cowed by authority than ever before. And we will have only ourselves to blame. (Nov. 22, 2004: A15. Reprinted with express permission of National Post Company, a CanWest partnership.)

I produced a considerable portion of this article for several reasons. First, it reveals a very common sentiment in public opinion and media discourse about law and leniency: tough law is the only way to control crime. In fact, jurisdictions with punitive justice systems — including Saskatchewan, Manitoba and many states in the United States — have relatively high youth crime problems. In reality, excessive punishment has never been shown to curb crime, much less instill an "incentive to stay on the straight and narrow." This is especially true for many marginalized kids, who have been punished all their lives in one form or another. Second, sentiments like those above are ignorant of the reality that the framework of the YCJA is public safety. In fact, the Act has considerable power to deal harshly with repeat young offenders. Third, the provisions of the Act that call for diversion and alternative measures are meant to treat young people with dignity and respect, a social justice orientation that, in the long run, creates a safer society than one that practises punitive justice across the board. Fourth, the sentiments are devoid of any sense of the effect of incarceration on young people. We know full well that incarceration leads to recidivism and incarceration. Harsh laws do not create moral authority — they create the context in which already dispossessed young people become further dispossessed.

In November 2004, the *Globe and Mail* reported on a young offender incident that resulted in the death of a fifty-two-year-old mother. The article entitled "Wild in the streets" (Nov. 12, 2004: A18) expressed concern that a repeat car thief was not placed in custody, drove through an intersection in a stolen car and killed a mother of three. The article lamented the fact that a recidivist car thief was an "out of control" youth, who should have been locked up. As with other articles of this sort, the blame for threats to public safety is placed squarely on the youth justice system for its leniency and its inability to punish adequately. Interestingly, the article does affirm that non-violent offenders should not be in custody, but this position is neutralized first by the alarmist headline and second by the article's insistence that crime cannot be neatly divided into violent and non-violent and that the Act must concentrate on designations of violence. A similar article appeared in the *National Post* in April 14, 2005, which focused on girls and violence. The article entitled "Violence by teenage girls still a concern, police say" revisits the Victoria, BC, Reena Virk murder of 1997 and quotes experts who reaffirm that violence amongst girls is still a concern and that vigilance is needed in a world of expanding female violence. The article does comment that actual rates of violence have decreased for girls overall, but the final summation declares, "Youth violence has always been with us but what has concerned us is the ethics of fighting and the intensity. To say youth violence numbers have come down doesn't mean we no longer need to be concerned and vigilant… as a society, we tend to turn a blind eye to aggression in girls" (A10).

Interestingly, like the article above, testimonials to the naturalness of youth violence are often found in articles about teenage murderers. Even without stating the innate violent nature of teenagers, such articles promote the suggestion that murder may be an ordinary activity for kids resulting from such innocuous psychological states as selfishness, low self-esteem, the need for thrills and high self-esteem. In the August 15, 1994, article in *Maclean's* entitled "Kids Who Kill," the three cases that are described in detail are typically about "The Boy across the Road" (37), "A Young Killer who Looked like a Choirboy and who had no Obvious Problems at Home" (38) and a "handsome, rather lanky youth" that people trusted so completely that "later that night he left the teen to baby-sit his own two young sons" (34). The three descriptions suggest that youth murder occurs in ordinary socio-economic contexts. The same type of writing occurs in an article embedded in the *Alberta Report* article (Dec. 6, 1993). The article entitled "Crimes Beyond Reason" (20) lists five cases of teenagers who killed

family members and premises the discussions by suggesting that "ever since Cain slew Abel, humanity has harboured men, women, and children who can, without real reason or remorse, strike down those they love the most" (20). The descriptions, once again, are rife with references to kids reacting violently for little more than petty theft or reaction to parental discipline, all the while communicating the feeling that ordinary kids kill for trivial reasons.

The techniques for endorsing moral panics in the articles I have discussed in this section are clever and subtle. The articles generally present alarmist headlines, followed by conjecture and scientific evidence that support a crime epidemic amongst youth. The ideological framework in the last few years is based on the logic of forensic science — that we can detect and understand delinquent young people because science, now more than ever, gives us the tools to do so. As I argue in the next chapter, the language of forensics now contains knowledge of race, culture, gender, gangs, genetic/congenital problems and risk/vulnerability. Most current news reports of youth crime draw upon these ideological orientations and produce compelling accounts of why young people are bad. In doing so, however, they miss very fundamental elements of crime and social justice. Despite all these types of forensic "knowledge," the fact remains that young people in trouble with the law generally live on the margins of society. The options we have for understanding youth crime are either to blame young people or to look at society's inability to accommodate them. I argue that relegation of blame to the individual (or the individual's immediate family or culture) — the essence of moral panics found in media accounts — is part of a larger agenda of condemnation of youth that has at its core the worldwide exploitation of children and youth in a global political economy.

Conclusion: Media, Decontextualization and Moral Panics

The examples analyzed above illustrate the different ways tin which public discourse has been framed in newspapers and newsmagazines. In analyzing moral panics, it is crucial to categorize how these accounts use individual examples as the norm, thereby decontextualizing criminal behaviour from the structured nature of society. When crime problems are framed in the context of morality, poor parenting and "poor people," they are reduced to the level of individual pathology and its moral connections to privation. The legitimacy of "normal," affluent lifestyles is reinforced, as is the legitimacy of the social order. In essence, the moral panic draws on public perceptions about crime and criminality and reinforces these beliefs by fomenting fear about the unpredictable and dangerous nature of youth activity.

The real connection between poverty and youth crime is not individual pathology but that marginalized youth are more vulnerable to commit certain crimes (street crime primarily) and are similarly more vulnerable to the scrutiny and control of the criminal justice system. As a society, we need to ensure that resources for marginalized kids are available, because as Monture-Angus (1996) argues, there is a distinction between disadvantaged and dispossessed. The problems of dispossessed or marginalized kids, like those described in this book, are economic, not moral. In a similar vein, Monture-Angus argues, people in Aboriginal communities tend to be relatively poor and unemployed, and yet they maintain a strong sense of community. On the basis of my research, I argue that the same can be said for dispossessed youth in general. As my interviews with marginalized youth over several years have shown, they tend to be loyal and generous, and have a strong sense of solidarity with one another. Their lived reality is, however, that they are caught more often than kids who are more affluent and mainstream.

This book shows that the groups who dominate the media — white, male, professional, capital-controlling classes — hold hateful, stereotypical views of youth misconduct. When they present these views, they obliterate other, more favourable images of youth, at the same time, claiming that there is no alternative to youth crime other than "tough" law and order. Those who dominate the media circumscribe the public debate about youth and the troubles they face.

CHAPTER 5

Criminalizing Marginality:
Creating Young Folk Devils

When the media write about youth crime and misconduct, they generally attack those who are marginalized or present their stories primarily in the context of the lives of such people. In so doing, they help create and foster a collective enmity towards the young, especially those who are already socially and economically disadvantaged. The existing disempowerment that racial minorities, women and the poor suffer at the hands of socio-economic and socio-legal systems is thereby exacerbated by media accounts of crime. William Ryan, in his landmark study, *Blaming the Victim* (1976), states: "difference is in itself hampering and maladaptive. The Different Ones are seen as less competent, less skilled, less knowing — in short less human" (10).

The importance of Ryan's work lies in his reminder that the already victimized are the most likely to be negatively labelled. Groups that are most vulnerable are those least likely to be able to resist public enmity and easily distinguishable from the dominant socio-economic strata. In typical media depictions of youth criminals, the categories for condemnation are consistent: poor families (living in poor communities); racially based gangs/groups (either recent immigrants or Aboriginal Canadians); and both single-mothers and mothers who work outside the home. The categories of race, class and gender often arise in sociological analyses in connection with discrimination and maltreatment, and the discursive creation of youth folk devils is no exception. It is interesting that in the context of media accounts of youth deviance, gang criminality is often a codeword identifier for a racialized group or the poor, while the criminogenic family is an identifier for poor families or families headed by single mothers.

I would like to stress at this point that many of the depictions that I analyze in this book border on hate literature. As an analytical device, in your reading of the examples, try substituting mainstream and powerful racial, socio-economic and gender categories for the ones being used. This technique should illustrate to you that hateful statements are only tolerated when directed at marginalized groups.

Public discourse during the 1990s was more blatant in its attempts to create folk devils out of young people in trouble with the law than is new millennium discourse. While media accounts have become more muted and covert, the underlying messages have not changed. The vitriol has been constant over the whole of the past fifteen years. Like discourse about other criminals, the discourse about youth offenders is a condemnation of those on the margins of society; young people in trouble with the law are condemned for being in single-mother families, for having non-white skin and for being poor.

The global view of children and youth has arguably reached a new level of condemnation. The form of that condemnation, at least in North America, has become more covert and at times almost metaphorical. The subtlety of post-millennium accounts is the result, in part, of the rhetoric of science. The code words embedded in the rhetoric certainly implicate children and youth as much as ever, but they do so in a language that condemns by association rather than by overt designation. The way in which we now talk about, and the issues which frame how we talk about, "bad kids" are partly reflective of our renewed investment in forensic science — the overall approach to crime that is based on issues of risk, vulnerability and control. The underlying theme of this "criminological" approach is that if you can figure out the nature of the criminal you can at the very least remove them from "decent" society and maintain the security and safety of decent citizens.

For example, the *Youth Criminal Justice Act* (2003) has, as its guiding principle, public safety. Although the Act contains provisions for diverting young offenders away from the court system and into community participation, the public safety framework is based on forensic detection and coercive control for extreme offenders. This orthodox, consensus approach to crime and justice reflects an old and enduring body of conservative theorizing that has at its core the quest to understand "the deviant." Although derivations of this consensus go beyond the individual to explore the societal bases of bad behaviour, they never really question how bad behaviour becomes defined, how justice is often the result of one's place in the socio-economic structure and how issues of good and evil become the bases for exploitation and marginalization. While the following discussion illustrates the somewhat new rhetoric of condemnation, much of the discourse is still characterized by blatancy and sensationalism.

The Risk of Delinquency:
Congenital Offenders and Congenital Families

The discourse of risk is closely intertwined with the discourse of sickness — especially congenital sickness — and the much more veiled discourse of maternal care. Within this line of forensic/health reasoning, we see the mixing of conservative and progressive spokespersons who, although they have different motives for their positions, seem to vie for the public's attention and belief. At the end of day, however, this medicalized discourse does what the language of criminality has done for centuries: it identifies and indicts the perpetrator as flawed, either biologically and/or culturally, and by consequence, morally flawed. While this type of socio-biological thinking is centuries old, the current form appears more scientifically supported and is more in keeping with the intuitive perceptions of the everyday person than the biologist orientations of the past. We identify cognitive disability with moral disability because we tend to privilege those who are successful, both educationally and financially. The nationwide attack on homelessness, for example, is a perfect indication of how we indict those who live on the margins of society for nothing more than being poor. Most urban jurisdictions in Canada have legislation to control the activities of street people. In fact, Ontario's *Safe Streets Act* is essentially an attack on poor kids, who are condemned for being on the street, and criminalizing panhandling and "squeegee kids," has further endangered the lives of street youth in Toronto (O'Grady and Greene 2003).

The thematic of congenitally bad kids connects their "sickness" to the family, to the community in which the child lives and most often, to the mother. While fetal alcohol syndrome (FAS), fetal alcohol effect (FAE) and fetal alcohol spectrum disorder (FASD) undoubtedly have a reality in some form, the fact that we have created a language that constructs the diagnosed in criminogenic terms tells us something about the way we view criminality and marginality. The debates often blame cognitive damage in children and youth on maternity and nutrition in relation to poverty and race. In public discourse about morality, mother-blaming predominates in some not so subtle ways.

An article in the *Calgary Herald* in 2004 explained youth crime through a myriad of individual and sub-cultural issues that included "poor parenting, age, gender, ethnicity, witnessing violence, difficulty in school, peer influences, alcohol abuse, Fetal Alcohol Syndrome Disorder/Fetal Alcohol Effects, and cognitive or personality traits" (May 6, 2004: N9). The article, "Poor parenting puts kids at risk," draws on the work of forensic scientists and police officers and presents a compelling argument that poverty is only one of the risk factors for delinquency, but that individual and familial attributes are the things that control morality. The article uses the medical model as the paradigm for understanding delinquency by incorporating a litany of characteristics that take the reader back to the individual. The article concludes by talking about risk and the need to assess delinquency, and in so doing, critiques the "one dimensional" model that focuses on economic marginality.

A second example illustrates how a more benevolent telling of the story of sick delinquent kids produces the same stigma as the more malevolent ones. In November 19, 2003, the *Saskatoon Star Phoenix* (A3) produced an article entitled "FASD situation 'bleak': Judge," based on comments by a local provincial court judge. The First Nations judge, having a reputation for being progressive and kind, articulated her frustration with the implementation of the new *Youth Criminal Justice Act*. The article described her dissatisfaction with a system that could not care adequately for damaged teens, only providing them with closed custody. Her sentiments concur with a host of like-minded individuals who lobby for better non-judicial treatment for dispossessed kids. The article, while attempting to appear progressive and sympathetic, uses the discourse of sickness and individual responsibility in a non-reflective way to blame and implicitly condemn.

The following statements (reprinted with express permission of Saskatoon Star Phoenix) from the article illustrate the common sentiment that frames judicial and non-judicial understandings of kids in trouble:

A Saskatoon teenager born with an alcohol-related brain defect faces a bleak future of incarceration instead of treatment because of lack of provincial government services for youth with FASD, a provincial court judge says. The sixteen-year-old boy was raised by a single mother who has severe alcohol and drug addiction that have led to the trauma for the boy, placement in foster homes and trouble with the law that has already landed him in closed custody facilities for more than a year.

It appears that no priority is given to meeting the needs of youth in the criminal justice system who suffer from FASD coupled with a traumatic background.

There are no firm statistics on the prevalence of FASD, but a 1996 Saskatchewan study estimated it is present in 24 to 30 live births per year.

Is he failing society's expectations or are we failing him by expecting too much in light of the FASD diagnosis?

Representatives of the provincial departments responsible for health, social services and corrections all describe numerous programs aimed at helping youth with FASD but they agree the issues surrounding it are complex and require a high level of co-ordination among departments that may not yet be in place.

The article discusses the reality that in Saskatchewan, and similarly in other provinces, 85 percent of government spending on corrections goes to custody and only 13 percent to community services. It paints a depressing picture of the courts' inability to meet the stated mandate of the *Youth Criminal Justice Act* to provide alternatives to incarceration. In a context of the withdrawal of social services funding, the courts are relegated to using custodial sentences that are characterized by confinement and detention.

I present this article and the above excerpts for two reasons. First, the article shows clearly that we do a very poor job of caring for dispossessed youth and that we do not have the imagination or the will to think outside the "custodial box" for young people. We are in the "habit of custody," and unfortunately, our use of custody is based on a philosophy that young offenders "get what they deserve." The people who speak out, like the justice officials in the article, are at the forefront of progressive commentary that, although badly needed, largely falls on deaf ears. For the purposes of this book, however, I present this article to show how the stigma of medical discourse "slips into" debates about marginal kids. We have become so inured to the belief system that individuals are the root of criminality that we do not stop to consider that kids in trouble could mostly be the result of a society unable to account for types of difference. The inability to sit still in school, to concentrate in a formal classroom context, to score well on an exam, to think at a high level of abstraction and to "pass" a psychological assessment may be in indicative of a child different from the norm but should certainly not be indicators of moral inferiority or even cognitive ability. The discourses of FASD, conduct disorder, ADHD, risk and vulnerability are all elements of forensic science as applied to children and youth, and they have become part of the discourses of criminality and intellectual ability. When, however, we strip away the language, the diagnoses and the labels, we are left with the incontrovertible reality that kids in trouble are dispossessed from the social structure — at a simpler level, they are relatively poor. As both conservative and progressive commentators focus on individual pathology, they ignore the pathology of inequality and they exonerate a society in which marginalized and dispossessed children and youth end up in custody for characteristics and activities that are about health, not crime. Medical discourse helps convert a public health problem into a problem of crime.

Articles such as this are very powerful ideological stories in that they convey the message that we can detect bad kids through a series of risk factors. The critique of risk is gaining more currency as justice policy officials use forensic knowledge to determine criminality. The modern neo-liberal political orientation, which pervades human rights programs in western industrial societies, is rife with notions of individual responsibility, individual risk and individual entrepreneurship (O'Malley 2000; Pratt 2000). And the risk assessment orientation of contemporary youth justice is consistent with neo-liberal philosophies. The problem is that in a paradigm in which healing and rehabilitation are still the expressed goals of justice, focusing on risk determines, by definition, that something wrong will be found. In fact, the expressed purpose of risk detection is to determine recidivism. The assessments never focus on individual or group potential, only liabilities — hence the term *risk*. Standardized assessments, such as the Level of Supervision Inventory (LSI), a risk assessment tool that has been adopted in one form or another in Canada and other countries as a mechanism for determining the type and level of intervention for young offenders, clearly cannot explore potential because they focus on deficiencies. Such tools are instruments that confirm the bad things in a person's life, an orientation that should be contradictory to philosophies of care and healing. The LSI assesses the following: criminal history, education/employment, family/marital issues, leisure/recreation issues, companions, substance abuse, pro-criminal attitude/orientation and anti-social patterns (Girard and Wormith 2004). As a predictor of criminal involvement, one cannot argue with its ability to do what is says it can, although the logic of the instrument is tautological — using criminality to predict criminality, risk to predict risk. Such as prediction of criminality can also be made by any commonsense judgment of a youth worker who understands the life of a dispossessed youth. The only thing the instrument does is lend the credibility of empirically based science to condemn the already condemned. In this "scientific atmosphere," it is understandable how news reports that frame delinquency in the context of individual pathology maintain their credibility.

One of the most significant dimensions of risk and individual pathology is the phenomenon of substance abuse. In a larger social context in which substance abuse, especially of alcohol and tobacco, are considered culturally acceptable, we ferret out young people as criminals who fall prey to using illicit substances. It is interesting and alarming, as well, that we do not frame youth substance abuse as a health problem instead of a crime problem. A perfect example of this surrounds the current panic over crystal meth, a street drug that is quickly addictive and easy to manufacture from over-the-counter cold medicine, and that has become a criminal identifier for delinquent youth. The Attorney-General of North Dakota, in a conference in Regina on the crystal meth epidemic in western North America, indicated that his state has had to build more prisons to deal with this new drug problem. Sixty percent of the males in the prison system in North Dakota are meth addicts and the budget for the North Dakota penitentiary system doubled over seven years. In his words, "We had to, in addition to that, construct a whole new women's prison, just for the women inmates, just about all of whom are there because of meth addiction problems, or meth manufacturing problems" (CBC.ca, June 10, 2005.) Clearly, politicians cannot, or will not, perceive drug use and abuse as problems of individual and collective health, opting instead to define them as a problem of crime. As well, the war on crystal meth use is primarily a war on use by children and youth, when the greatest proportion of abusers of illegal and legal drugs is adults (Males 2000). While drug abuse is serious for young and old, the attack and the ensuing public panic places the young "offender" at the centre.

Blaming Mothers and Families at the End of the Millennium

The discussions in this section take us back several years to the mid to late 1990s. The depictions illustrate that the generalized public talk about crime and its connection to family and motherhood have been in vogue for a decade or more. Clearly here, both the most overt and most subtle forms of hatred are direct attacks on women, motherhood, and the poor. Like the discussions of risk, the rhetoric of the 1990s is couched in circumspect language that often laments the states of privation in which many people live. When we look deeper, we can see that the subtle images and messages, like those in discussions of forensic science, imply that while poverty may not be a matter of choice, single mothers are responsible for their socio-economic and marital conditions and that they are the most likely to produce criminal children through their own negligence. Rarely do accounts of poor mothering mention the responsibility of the father, of the society in which women's work is devalued and underpaid, or the under-funded system of social justice, which herds kids in and out in attempts to cope with diminishing resources. The offenders and victims are quite distinct, and mothers who live below the poverty line are clearly constructed as either inadvertent or deliberate offenders.

Poverty and the Pathological Family

One category of media depictions is based on surprisingly accurate descriptions of life for young offenders. These presentations focus on trying to understand the social and personal origins of youth crime and in this regard seem to be quite progressive in their approaches. The hidden messages, however, come to light as the articles venture further into the realm of personal responsibility for crime. A *Calgary Herald* article illustrates how a factual accounting of and for crime can place the blame for criminal behaviour on the most vulnerable people in society. The article omits any discussion of the structural origins of problem kids by focusing on abuse within the home, without discussing why abuse occurs and why dysfunctional families are ones that exist below the poverty line.

> Any child can kill, but there is a disturbing trend among those who do. They are often abused, neglected or unwanted. Their homes are run more like hotels with parents not bothering if they check in or out. They wander the streets and wind up stealing car stereos or burglarizing homes — often because there's nothing better to do. They don't express their feelings, they grow up seeing people as objects and they can't differentiate right and wrong. And then they kill. (*Calgary Herald*, Aug. 9, 1990: C3)

The excerpt and article present an alarmingly stereotypic view of youth crime. The chronological listing of the development of criminal behaviour reads like a psychiatrist's report, preceded by the absurd statement that any child can kill. One thing necessarily leads to another, which leads to another patterned response, which leads to emotional flatness, which leads to murder. In this development of the killer personality, the blameworthy are without question the families, who do not want their children, who do not care where they are and who abuse them. These stereotypes are numerous in news reports, and as I contend throughout this book, they are often wrong.

The article then presents a short list of murders by youth and culminates with a statement by unspecified "experts":

> Criminologists and psychologists agree that raising a child who kills can happen to families from all walks of life, but families that are barely surviving — the welfare mom in East Vancouver, the newly arriving immigrant to Surrey — are more likely to see it in their homes. (C3)

The article draws on public fears and stereotypes to make its point: the criminogenic families are headed by single mothers and immigrants. The not-so-subtle implication is that these families produce killers, for that is what the article is about. That these bold statements are untrue and unsupported makes them racist and sexist in their indictment of women and immigrants. The article finishes with a powerful statement by an unidentified criminologist, who implies that all teenagers from "unstable families" are potentially criminal: "You have someone in a high state of arousal, confusion, with the hormones percolating. They are very, very susceptible especially if they're from an unstable background" (C3). The article has come full circle from an opening statement about the human condition, that any child can kill, to a similar bio-determinist avowal that puberty and hormonal changes create lethal kids, especially if such kids live in poverty.

From the Crime of Poverty to the Criminality of Single Motherhood

The foregoing article shows quite clearly the quick evolution of blame from poverty to family to motherhood. The James Bulger murder case, which I discussed in Chapter 4, similarly illustrates how attempts to be fair-minded by presenting an abundance of possible reasons for horrific crimes slips easily into a focus on mothers and families as the root of youth evil. One of the children was described as "the classic product of a broken home" (*Daily Mail*, November 25, 1993). In typical sensationalist fashion, London newspapers went on a rampage of speculation as to the connections between a horrific youth crime and underclass, female-headed families. Related stories concentrated on a mother with seven children who smoked, dyed her hair, drank and had boyfriends.

The implication in the London papers was that children left to single mothers (or families with absentee fathers) are potential killers. The most harmful sentiment to arise from anti-mother accounts of youth crime is that society needs to be vigilant in watching for the signs of criminality, and the British papers, reporting on the Bulger case, provided the markers of family criminality, including single-motherhood, divorce/separation, poverty and parents who indulge in vices. In fact, the two boys who killed Bulger were not at all typical of children of separated or divorced parents.

From Single Motherhood to the Crime of Feminism

The discourse of mother-blaming has a natural ally in the discourse of feminism-blaming. This reality is exemplified by an example I used earlier based on the cover story in *Alberta Report*. Recall the visual depiction of a young girl brandishing a gun under a caption that reads "Killer Girls." The visual nature of the account notwithstanding, the article is significant in its flagrant claim that women's struggle for gender equality is at the core of criminality. This blatantly prejudicial narrative is given credibility by invoking the statements of those who should be most upset by the absurdities therein.

> If mothers have always observed the unfamiliar pursuits of their adolescent daughters with mingled suspicion and anxiety, they have good reason to feel nauseated today. Impelled by contemporary culture, their daughters are becoming not just difficult, but often violent and ruthless monsters. That was dramatically highlighted

earlier this month, when three Calgary girls were charged in the brutal stabbing death of a Calgary man.... Modern women may have no one to blame but themselves, however. Girls, after all, are only following their foremothers' lead in seizing the torch of the 1970s feminist cults of androgyny and victimhood and torquing it up to new extremes. And as they abandon traditional feminine domains for once-masculine arenas like commerce and politics, they are increasingly emulating less savory male models — such as murderers and maimers. As American feminist novelist Katherine Dunn unapologetically puts it: "Being equal means being equally bad and equally good." (1995: 24)

This article is especially noteworthy in its attempts to link criminality with the "dark side" of femaleness, the unnatural desire to be like men, prompted by feminism. The article is framed around a "cult of female violence," whose spokeswomen are Courtney Love and Roseanne Barr.

By posing two showbusiness people as icons of the modern violent woman, the article indicts women who are in control and who defy traditional female roles, even though in the case of Love and Barr, the defiance is most certainly done for entertainment value. The accompanying pictures show grunge rock singer Love in a seductive, defiant pose with the caption, "Tormented trollop Love: Driven by Testosterone" (27). In the case of TV sitcom star Barr, the camera has captured her in a particularly evil-looking pose, with the caption, "Roseanne: Just call me a killer bitch" (27). While the article ignores that these are contrived media images, it is callous in its statements regarding the male-like nature of bad girls. Love is "the tortured grunge queen with the testosterone fixation," and Barr says "I think women should be more violent, kill more of their husbands" (27). The imputation is that Love and Barr are feminists who condone violence. But more important than these almost silly references to media personages are the hateful references in this article, for example, to Love a trollop, as an "unrivalled tough slut," to her singing as "retching," are indications of the lengths to which magazines and newspapers will go to seduce readers. The inflammatory language in the article is typical in that it is intended to raise aversive passions in the reader, to engender an unquestioning belief that we are on the march to self-destruction and to make us aware that violent teens are the torch bearers.

The article reinforces its arguments through varied and bizarre testimonials intended to "prove" that what is being said is incontrovertible. Authors, identified as feminist commentators, are quoted out of context throughout the article, lamenting that traditional femaleness is dying:

today's teenagers are rejecting their female nature altogether. They have turned against the idea of what it is to be a woman; Women are not sequestered in their kitchens as they used to be. As a result our crimes are no longer limited to poisoning our husbands and abusing our children. We can hitchhike across the country killing people. We can drive off on an armed robbery spree. (24)

The President of the Canadian Police Association is quoted as saying that though "females in general have achieved equality... the downside of that is that they are much more active in crime." Both statements are unsubstantiated and inaccurate claims. The article further claims that "such an outcome was not an entirely unexpected consequence of female emancipation." In a rather outlandish addition to the litany of professional testimonials, the article quotes Queen Victoria:

"Woman would be the most hateful, heartless and disgusting of human beings were she allowed to unsex herself," the British monarch wrote in an 1870 letter. Her prediction has been borne out, Mr. Racho acknowledges ruefully: "It is sad to note how each advance seems to make women more unsatisfied, more spiteful, and more vulgar.... Indeed some of the crimes by modern girls seem every bit as vulgar as any perpetrated by men." (25)

Using the technique of providing a list of cases that proves the point, the article describes a series of schoolyard cases involving violence and voices of young male counterparts affirming that "females can outdo the most savage male" (25).

Articles such as this in *Alberta Report* make the connection between the struggle for gender equality and youth crime and, by implication, indict strong women as a social evil. The implications are clear and rather common: that women who choose to go outside of the home are a social risk; that mothers are mostly responsible for child-rearing and are to blame when children go wrong; that there is an unpredictable natural female essence; that traditional femininity is lost when calculating women decide to shrug off their natural familial duties; and that if we wish to detect predelinquency, we had better study the home and especially the quality and degree of maternal care.

In a more current body of work that studies the growing public panic over the crimes of girls and women, one of the prevailing findings is that public discourse is based on the often expressed assumption that girls are engaging in horrific crimes in unprecedented numbers and that the explanations must lie somewhere in the struggle by girls and women for gender equality. Bell (2002) shows quite clearly how a few violent cases of young girl violence become beacons for public panic. And, as with many media accounts of youth crime, experts express the need for panic in excessive and alarmist terms:

> According to veteran police officers, the details of some girls attacks are too horrifying to retell. "Believe me, you don't want to know," a police sergeant reportedly commented about one case. "It was horrifying," said the veteran of over twenty-eight years on the force. He had seen assaults and robberies over the years but never anything like that one.... Law enforcement officials often cited as experts on the crisis, say that girls are "more likely than boys to use firearms," and other "authorities" on girls' violence make claims that "girls are often more ruthless and aggressive than their male counterparts. (Bell 2002: 130)

High profile crimes like the Reena Virk murder in Victoria and the murder by Serena Nicotine of a half-way house worker in North Battleford, Saskatchewan, seem to be watershed cases for the recent public panic over girls' criminality. I discuss the Virk case in a subsequent section but suffice it to say that such cases become negative cultural symbols for all that is bad about modern society and modern young people. The discussions are often laden with rampant speculation about modern morality, feminism and the rise of the modern women struggling for equality with men. The news medium, with its inherent prejudices about a simple, bifurcated world and its penchant for controlled editorializing, has much to say about the nature of gender and modern morality. Faith and Jiwani (2003) studied high profile criminal cases by women/girls, including the Virk murder, and show quite clearly how media monopolies, corporations that are owned and controlled by "white, upper-class men," frame female crime in an androcentric tradition that focuses on a "female proclivity" to violence. The ideological mould on which female crime is built is one of women struggling for gender equity. As Faith and Jiwani rightly argue: "In focusing on these women's transgressions, the media reinforce the normative social and moral order. They imply the rewards that accrue if women 'stay in their place'" (Faith and Jiwani 2003: 104).

Race and Youth Crime: Gang Talk and Cultural Collision

The "Killer Girls" example I used in the preceding section on images of women is spotted throughout with references to gangs. But as in most media articles, the gang is never defined in "Killer Girls." Rather, gang is used loosely to refer to kids who "hang around" in two or threes and who have an identifiable ethnicity or class. In fact, this article relates an incident in which a girl in Edmonton was "surrounded by 10 native girls who pushed her to the ground, kicked her and punched her in the face and stole her leather 'bomber' jacket" (*Alberta Report*, July 31, 1995: 25).

The panic over gangs that is typified by this article has been well-documented, especially in British research. Cohen's landmark work (1980) alerted us to the prospect that public actors like politicians, business people and the media have the potential to define, identify and scapegoat relatively vulnerable, highly identifiable people. For my purposes, there are two important issues in media discourse surrounding gangs: first, the potential terror that resides in kids "hanging around in groups," a phenomenon that is, ironically, typical of adult society; and second, the imputed relationships between gangs, specifically gang violence, and racialized or immigrant groups.

Between January 22 and 26, 2004, the *Saskatoon Star Phoenix* conducted a series of articles on gangs in Saskatchewan and, much like the gang references I describe in Chapter 4, these articles have overt visual and verbal referents to racialized youth, including a picture of a young Aboriginal male and the use of gang names such as the "Crazy Cree" and the "Indian Posse." The headlines that structured the stories were highly condemnatory and fear inducing: "Gangs feed on anger, thrive on brutality" (Jan. 24, 2004: A1); "Gangs' random violence puts public in great danger" (Jan. 23, 2004: A1).

Articles such as these construct public opinion in several ways. First, they relate gang activity to race and leave the public with only two referents: Aboriginal kids and evil gangs. The masking function is quite clear: issues of poverty, dispossession, social inequality, judicial unfairness and social isolation, all leave the landscape of public consciousness. Second, they create a crime control context in which increased law and order are the only ways to create a safe society, a proposal that has been consistently shown to be futile (Cayley 1998; Christie 2000, 1993).

The crime control message that emanates from public panics engenders considerable fear in the public and implies that individuals must become entrepreneurial in their own safety. A considerable body of literature that focuses on risk argues quite appropriately that the atmosphere of fear in the new millennium is one in which individuals feel that they, more so than in the past, must take control of their own safety. Complementary attitudes include a fear of adolescents, especially certain kinds of adolescents, and support for simple criminal justice measures that remove bad kids from society. It is significant that gangs are conceptualized by the public as something derived from bad kids living in bad cultures. In Saskatchewan, gangs are perceived as essentially an Aboriginal problem rather than a problem of a poorly functioning, non-egalitarian society that is ill at all levels. What is noticeable about the discriminatory sentiments expressed in the *Star Phoenix* report are the references to gang experts and gang research. And some of the experts are members of visible minority communities that are the targets of the reports; that experts are taken from inside and outside the community lends legitimacy to the accounts.

Even in the more even-handed reports of gang activity, the legacy of news reporting to date determines relatively biased, highly presumptive accounts. On December 3, 2005, the *Winnipeg Free Press* reported that four "gang members" attacked some youth in a local high school with mace and then fled. The theme of the story was that it was "youth against youth" and that the perpetrators were organized gang members. The first line of the front page story, entitled "Gang hits Tuxedo school" (Dec. 3, 2005: F1), was, "Inner city gang members invaded Tuxedo' Shaftesbury High School." After describing the incident, the story stated that the police were unsure whether the assailants were linked to gangs, but then proceeded to discuss a certain gang called "Mad Cowz." The "Mad Cowz" gang is associated with recent immigrant young people from Africa, and the story suggests that they prey on and recruit new immigrants. The race and immigration issues are interspersed with language that refers several times to an "invasion" of an ordinary upper-middle-class school and to police responding in their mandate to protect nice communities from "invasion." It is entirely possible that the violence that the story relates is about a drug deal gone wrong in this wealthy high school; those students have money to buy drugs. The story also produced an insert with a list of four "recent" incidents involving gangs in schools since 2001, a phenomenon of less than one incident a year in a city of Winnipeg's large size.

Most certainly, the community has the right to address violence in schools, and of course parents are concerned for their children's safety. However, certain ideas muddy this journalistic account and actually stand in the way of determining the source and the solution to violence. First, the presumption is that the assailants are youth and, by implication, the incident is a youth problem. Nowhere is this verified. A follow-up article the next day described the attackers as "four teenagers wearing baseball caps" (*Winnipeg Free Press*, Dec. 4, 2005: A5) — baseball being somehow relevant to depictions of young people. Second, the overall sense is that this was an incident of organized gangs. The article uses the term "gang" both in its headline and through statements made by parents and teachers.

Quite clearly, the gang discourse evokes strong stereotype-based passions in the reader. Again, the history is presented in a context containing very few "facts" and in which gang experts are called upon to verify the accounts.

Despite the fact that the incident occurred in a school, the discourse in this article is about bad kids and organized gangs. It appears that the only way we can talk or think about such behaviour is within the context of the world that adolescents inhabit. So, schools, the daily habitat of adolescents, are transformed in media coverage of rare events into breeding grounds for violent behaviour, crime, non-conventional dress and other stereotypical attributes associated with being a teenager. The media do not report the more common daily activities of children and adolescents in school, some of which are dreadfully dull for young people and some of which attest to their better natures. It is almost as if we have no other way of talking about young people than to talk about their violence and victimization, racialized badness and the deterioration of the culture of school.

It is important to contextualize this story in the socio-economic reality of a city like Winnipeg. It is defensible that the incident described in the article is newsworthy, in part, because the fight was at an upper-middle-class, mostly white school. Similar fights happen in inner city, racially diverse schools all the time and never get media attention, all of which shows the deep racism of the media discourse about gangs. The basic presumption is that the event is newsworthy because it is so atypical of "good" schools in "good" areas of the city.

Another example, from Saskatoon in October 1995, illustrates how the press, in compliance with the police and courts, overreacts to and exaggerates teenage gang activity and relates such activity to visible minorities. The city police issued a press release suggesting that criminal gangs were becoming a problem in the city and that the gangs were racially based and comprised of relatively young people. The estimate in the initial press release was that twelve gangs existed in the city and that they were engaged in drug use and the sex trade; the alarm was sounded that the police did not have the staff or the skills to deal with the situation. After a visit to police and civic officials from a youth gang specialist from Winnipeg, the *Saskatoon Star Phoenix* carried an article that discussed police complaints of organized youth gangs whose activities were restricted to the downtown core. The article, entitled "Street gangs reality in city" (*Saskatoon Star Phoenix*, November 4, 1995: A1, A2), reported the evidence for the gang presence, including graffiti advertising "gang-related" sentiments and an increase in sports jackets thefts. The article expressed the uncertainty surrounding gang activity and speculated on the danger of gangs reaching maturity in the city. The article caused a good deal of public furore and prompted civic and police officials to declare a police task force to pre-empt gang violence.

The report illustrates how journalists uses speculation and half truths to create an atmosphere of alarm, while inserting a series of disclaimers that indicate that the information may not be true. Consider, however, the chronology of presentations in this article create an aura of fact from uncertain information. The article begins:

> Indian Posse. White Supremacists. Cowboys. Indie Boys. West Side Divas. Luckys. Flips. These are street-gang names, and they're not from Los Angeles or New York. Nor are they from Vancouver or Toronto. And they're not from Calgary or Winnipeg either. They're from Saskatoon.

The writer suggests that at least seven and likely more organized gangs exist in Saskatoon. Later on the retractions begin:

> The full extent of street-gang activity in the city is an open question.... All that remains of gangs in the downtown corridor now is the distinctive graffiti sprayed on brick walls and written on doorways.... The police will not publicly confirm the names of the gangs for fear of legitimizing something that may not exist.... There are wildly divergent estimates of how many gangs members are on the streets in Saskatoon. They range from in the low 20s to as many as 300.

Quite unapologetically, this article presents a social problem as established fact in both the headline and the opening statements and then distances itself from the assertion. Approximately one week later, after the panic had subsided, the *Saskatoon Star Phoenix* printed an article based on new evidence from the police force that there were at most only two gangs in Saskatoon, that they were loosely organized, that they likely did not have ties to organized crime and that they did not pose a significant policing problem. An unsubstantiated alarm over youth crime had for a short period of time created a reality that aroused fear in citizens and condemned inner city youth. This example is significant because it illustrates that a public alarm over youth crime can arise quickly, that the press is significant in fostering such a panic and that people tend to ignore the lies and exaggerations as harmless mistakes.

Several other things are noteworthy in this Saskatoon example. First, the police were fulfilling a mandate to be prepared for a risk to public safety. In their enthusiasm to do the right thing, they sounded an alarm that reverberated throughout the community, and in their desire to adequately warn the public, they flagrantly exaggerated the extent of gang violence. Second, by focusing on the downtown area, the police, as is often the case with the youth justice system, turned the problem of gang violence into one of geography, race and class. Like all typical, relatively affluent Canadian cities, Saskatoon's youth violence, gang membership and vandalism/graffiti are not restricted to inner city areas. In fact, the affluent areas of such cities report rather high levels of defiant and deviant behaviours amongst youth. But as in all moral panics, the targets of the community's collective hostility were marginalized, inner-city, ethnically identifiable youth. Ultimately, "gang" becomes a racist code word in the media to refer to Aboriginal and immigrant kids. Third, the press were more than willing to partake of the debate, thus illustrating an essential quality of a thriving moral panic: cooperation between the media and agencies of social control. Last, it is significant that the claims regarding youth crime and gang membership gained credibility when the debate was endorsed by experts. Whether or not experts understand the singular circumstance, their opinions on the topic generally suggests that the concern must be legitimate. The expert on gangs in this case addressed issues of organized crime, exploitation of children and gang culture — all topics that have currency and relevancy in Canadian society. That these issues are important and deserving of public attention is not in dispute. The expert opinion in question, however, presented in an atmosphere of paranoia about young offenders, shifted the focus from adult crime and issues of child welfare to young gang members. Once again, it is conceivable that the best intentions of public officials and social control agents resulted in a constructed malevolence for young people.

Media reports include sweeping unsubstantiated but condemnatory statements about gang behaviour: "members of fashion conscious youth gangs that police say are now established at virtually every high school in Southern Ontario" (*Globe and Mail*, Toronto, Metro Edition, May 23; 1990: A1, A2); "The flap of the [YOA] act comes at a time when violent youth crime is on the rise and cities are plagued with street gangs" (*Montreal Gazette*, Apr. 8, 1989: B1); youth gang activity in Ottawa apparently "mirrored a wave of crime committed by youthful gang members that afflicts cities across Canada" (*Maclean's*, May 18, 1992: 35). Vague and generic statements about gang-related activity often include the use of the word "gang" to refer to small groupings of kids, especially pre-teens: "two gangs of 11-year-old grade six students" and "three 10-year-old boys physically accosted a nine-year-old and stripped him of his running shoes" (*Maclean's*, May 18, 1992: 35).

It is important to state that when youth gang violence occurs, it is un-

deniably a problem in need of intervention. And I do not mean to trivial-
ize the problem. I do wish to suggest that the "plague" of gang violence is
an acute exaggeration We need look no further than some very credible
work on girls and gangs to see that gang membership has a structural reality
that needs investigation and explication. Melanie Nimmo's study on girls
and gangs for the Canadian Centre for Policy Alternatives (Nimmo 2001)
provides us with an insightful, research-grounded study on the functional
nature of girls' gang membership as she explicates the security and sense
of empowerment that gangs provide. Nimmo also shows the dark side of
gang life, including involvement in the drug trade and violence as normative
behaviour. She presents a balanced study that demystifies the criminality of
gang members, debunks the myths of predatory criminals and de-romati-
cizes the popular culture image of the noble "gangster." The study provides
a much needed antidote to the popular cultural image of the gang as a place
where criminal individuals gather to facilitate their criminal activity. The
interview narratives provide us with an account of the humanity and the
reality of gangs: "they don't feel like they belong anywhere. So it gives them
a sense of belonging, that family. And you'll hear that from the girls, 'This
is my family' (9)"; "in spite of the violence and the negatives, and the illegal
activities, our kids tend to feel a sense that someone really wants them. . .and
the saddest part is that allegiance goes nowhere" (12). While it is true that
the majority of gang members are poor, of Aboriginal ancestry (in provinces
like Manitoba and Saskatchewan) and do come from dysfunctional, marginalized families, the enlightened position is to understand how marginality
and dispossession based on social traits foster the phenomenon of the gang.

Unfortunately, the image of gang members in the media is based on
popular cultural biases about class, race and family background that both
foster and play into already existing prejudices. The concept of the "gang"
has become a linguistic referent or a codeword that fosters powerful visceral reactions against visible minority youth and street kids. When news
accounts of gang activity discuss the membership, rituals and criminal activity, they either deliberately or inadvertently neglect to discuss the social
and economic reasons why kids congregate in rebellious groups, why affiliation is so important to young people. The ethical implications of branding
all youths who are in groups, especially in public settings like "the mall," as
potentially dangerous are completely ignored. When one clears away the
ideological smoke and mirrors, it is perfectly understandable that membership in gangs for marginalized and disaffiliated kids — or any kids for
that matter — is a simple, collective way to invest their lives with meaning.
Notwithstanding the probability that most adults prefer to congregate as
well, the unspecific and unbound use of the term "gang" in media accounts

contributes considerably to the public panic about kids out of control. One of the most insidious outcomes of such linguistic referencing is the targeting and scapegoating of visible minorities.

A blatant use of the linguistic reference to race occurs with the use of headlines using excessively large and emboldened print. Once again, the racial epithet is highly generic and is only used with reference to visible minority youth: "The crooked credit card capital: Calgary City Police blame surging fraud on the City's Asian gangs" (*Alberta Report*, September 21, 1992: 22), and "New insights into Alberta's Asian crime scene: The publicity angers Edmonton's Viets, but police say people have to know how extensive it is" (*Alberta Report*, October 26, 1992: 22). Both headlines illustrate attempts to provide readers with a context for reading the articles: youth gang violence is racial, restricted to Asians and well-organized.

I think that the most outrageous use of "word-based images" I encountered in my research was in a series of articles in the *Winnipeg Free Press* dealing with Winnipeg's burgeoning youth gang problem. One of the articles, a full page spread, entitled "Angry, bitter kids flex their muscles: An outsider's guide to youth gangs (*Winnipeg Free Press*, September 29, 1994: B1), contained a pictorial guide to the gangs in Winnipeg, with an sketched portrait of a typical gang member and a list of identifiable characteristics including racial composition, which was either Aboriginal or racially-mixed. It is interesting to note that when racial referents are unclear, the term used is "mixed racial" or "racially diverse," never white. This particular article is noteworthy and especially malevolent in its presentation of a poem written by an Indian Posse member to describe the activities and the criminological orientation of Aboriginal youth. The emboldened headline is "Your racist blood we will spill," and the poem reads as follows:

> The marching feet of the Indian Posse echoes in your mind,
> getting stronger day by day.
> Our colour is red and it's here to stay, some of us have
> something to prove and some of us already have.
> But all in all we are the Indian Posse and together we stand tall.
> We are a breed that has seen it all and had its better
> days, but in the end we will learn our true native ways.
> We are warriors and in our mind we will survive the war path.
> In the days of old, our people used to fight and kill each
> other and, as they did, we will if there is no other way.
> We hold our heads high because we are not scared to die for
> one another, for we will join the Great Spirit in the sky.
> Call us what you will, but it is your racist blood we will spill.
> —Brothers Forever: Indian Posse

The use of this essentially pictorial device is noteworthy for several reasons. First, of all the sentiments expressed in the poem, the newspaper chose to use the one inflammatory statement as the headline, despite the fact that the poem contains many other important and socially significant sentiments. Second, the poem is centred in the middle of the page under the large heading "Bad boys," and after the primary headline, it is the first thing the reader sees. Cursory consumers, who see only what is stark and highly visible, will no doubt come away with a sense of fear of and disdain for Aboriginal youth.

In general, racial references serve both journalistic and ideological purposes. They promote the image of the young offender as unlike the average viewer/reader, and in doing so, they create identifiability in the stereotype of the young offender. Such images play on already existing racialized biases in the community and use these biases to create anxiety in the reader. It is alarm that sells. Race-based images of gangs and young offenders predominate in the news because they help sell particular accounts. More distressingly, such comments help formulate societal opinions and attitudes toward "young folk devils." I reiterate that the use of race as a category of identification — especially when it is done in a consistently selective manner — serves no social purpose other than to create negative associations between racial characteristics and potential dangerousness.

The focus on criminality and race also masks, very dramatically, the fundamental reality in Canadian society that racism is often at the core of gang violence. The powerful sentiments expressed in the poem above show quite clearly that the Indian Posse and other Aboriginal gangs have a political consciousness that is based on cultural pride, on the struggle for race equity and on a sense of cultural solidarity. They use the bad boy image of the gang as a way of staring back at the gaze of racism of white Canadian society (Kelly 1998), as an antidote to the daily racism that characterizes their lives. In our study of kids in gangs in Saskatoon, my colleagues and I found a similar collective dynamic for very young kids, who wear certain colours and profess association with Aboriginal gangs. Their bravado and their pride in gang membership is fundamentally intertwined with their very basic human need to be accepted, to be secure and to withstand the day-to-day subtle and overt forms of racism that are endemic in the inner city core of highly racialized cities like Saskatoon (Lafontaine, Acoose and Schissel 2005).

The Crime of Being Poor

It is quite obvious that the discourse of news is replete with highly potent words that are a code for stereotypical representations. For example, when news accounts use the word "gang," the latent image is often one of members of visible minorities who live in poor urban areas. Such messages are often accompanied by pictures. Similarly, when depictions of youth crime refer to family disruption, they frequently focus on single-mothers or derelict mothers as responsible for youth misconduct. The "family problems" code phrase indicts the poor parenting of single mothers, decontextualized from economy or society, as the singular cause of youth malevolence. Equally important is the sub-textual connection between crime and poverty. Here I argue that the whole culture of criminal representation is based on subtle and embracing messages that the poor are not only responsible for crime but that *poverty is crime*. The isomorphic connection between poverty and badness is embedded in the codes of media discourse, and I illustrate how these code words infiltrate acceptable vernacular.

It is not just in articles about young offenders that the crime-poverty connection is made. Magazines and newspapers often carry accusatory articles about youth that are essentially poverty-bashing, especially targeting those who are dependent on social support. Welfare mothers, indigent and absentee fathers, youths on social support and the able-bodied who collect unemployment insurance all receive public censure through the voices of politicians and right-wing activists, who gain access to the public's attention through news media. The concept of "work for welfare," for example, is emblazoned with the ideological message that if people are physically capable of working, then they must either voluntarily or involuntarily be employed. Of course, this rhetoric is hollow given that many single-mothers are fully employed caring for their families, that laid-off workers have difficulty finding work, especially when economies are stagnating, and that it is not easy for needy citizens to face food bank line-ups or suffer the scrutiny of the social welfare system.

All this occurs within the context of rampant child poverty. Recall from Chapter 1, the extent of child poverty in Canada — something the federal government promised many years ago to eradicate by the turn of the century. They have not even come close. It is appalling — maybe even "criminal" — that a country as wealthy as Canada can have such a large group of people who have so little control over this aspect of their lives, who live below the poverty line.

Not surprisingly, the moral panic against the poor is most incessant when economies are suffering and when governments face what they portray as insurmountable budgetary deficits. A perfect example of how being both poor and young gets translated into blame occurred several years ago when the Saskatchewan NDP Government took a particularly non-enlightened stance on social assistance and labour. In early 1996, Premier Romanow declared that work for welfare would not be a part of the government's agenda for reducing the deficit, except for adolescents. This particular social democratic government declared that only youths would be singled out for welfare scrutiny, under the implication that families should be mandated to care for their adolescents. Similarly, in 1996, the government of British Columbia reduced welfare support to adolescents in favour of mandatory job searches, and Ontario legislated that sixteen and seventeen-year-olds on welfare had to be under adult supervision. Although the youths in question are of the age of consent and are legally citizens, their youth status and their economic need places them in the path of condemnation.

In a more recent vein, provincial governments across Canada are moving to workfare programs, which will hit young people especially hard because they are, in the eyes of the public, the able-bodied, undeserving poor (Shragge 1997; Hunter and Miazdyck 2006). Programs such as the McDonald's Bill in the United States — which allows businesses to pay young people 20 percent less than minimum wage (Schlosser 2002) — and France's proposed youth legislation bill — which permits the firing without cause of young people under the age of twenty-six — are clear examples that the general public believes that young people are undeserving of the rights that accrue to adults. It is important to note that policies that are in fundamental violation of the civil liberties of young people are implemented by both left- and right-wing governments.

The formalized occupational jeopardy within which young people live is starkly evidenced by the National Anti-Poverty Organization, presented in a press release by the International Labour Organization, which found that the first ones to be hit by downturns in the economy are the young, who consistently have a higher unemployment rate than older adults (ILO 2004). My lament is that policies that attack the young are part of the overall public panic against youth and are likely to drive kids onto the street, where they may face exploitation at the hands of adults.

From an analytical perspective, it is the combination of being young and being poor that surfaces in news media discourse. Several examples that I presented in *Blaming Children* illustrate the newsprint medium's condemnation of poverty and the associated issues of women and motherhood, ethnicity and innately evil young people. An article in the *Calgary Herald* is curiously a story about a retraction of an obvious attack on mothers and poverty. The article, entitled "Moms furious at MLA's betrayal: Tory calls single mothers vindictive leeches" (*Calgary Herald*, Apr. 18, 1995: A2), describes a verbal attack by an Alberta Member of the Legislative Assembly on single mothers in need who try to collect child support from fathers. The article is based on Premier Ralph Klein's admonition to the MLA that such statements are not appropriate for elected officials. The article goes on to discuss the plight of single mothers. However, most of the article discusses the unfair burden imposed on divorced fathers for child support. This article is noteworthy for two reasons. First, the headline contains, in bold letters, the condemnatory phrase by the MLA and a cursory reader sees only the visual connection between single mothers and social leeches. Second, although the article is about the inappropriateness of the comment by the MLA, the Premier's condemnation of the statement is dealt with in a nonchalant manner and quickly abandoned. The rest of the article concentrates on the discrimination suffered by fathers who are required to pay child support.

While this article contains no references to youth crime, it illustrates the ideology that forms an important backdrop to news articles that use poverty and motherhood as part of the calculus of crime. It indicates that highly placed individuals can attack, almost with impunity, categories of people who are seen or defined as assailable.

Other media accounts make the link between crime and poverty by attacking public policy and the principles of welfare. This excerpt from *Alberta Report* (May 2, 1994: 39) is a consummate example:

> Welfare dependency has also contributed to youth crime and family breakdown. Former Alberta crown attorney Scott Newark, now head of the Ottawa-based Canadian Resource Centre for Victims of Crime, argues, "Welfare is not a responsible way of dealing with young people who can just as easily work." It invites trouble by creating a "lifestyle that is fundamentally anti-social. Idleness is not a good thing." Mr. Newark believes that if young males are forced to support themselves, most will find work and the time they have to contemplate criminal behaviour will evaporate.
>
> Sociologists June O'Neill and Anne Hill of Baruch College of the City University of New York seem to have proven this empirically. In their study of inner-city poor, Professors O'Neill and Hill found that the higher the welfare payments, the greater the "negative effects on the behaviour of young men by increasing the likelihood of fathering a child out of wedlock, criminal activity, and by reducing their attachment to the labour force." The duo ultimately concluded that "a 50% increase in the monthly dollar value of welfare benefits led to a 117% increase in the crime rate among young black men." Such reasoning is, in part, behind Social Services Minister Mike Cardinal's announcement in early April that he wants the 29,000 singles still on welfare in Alberta to be off the rolls by the year 2000.

This excerpt illustrates how absurd the argument is that crime is caused by welfare rather than by poverty, disadvantage, job discrimination, over-policing and differential access to education. The decontextualized logic presented as empirically true by two American professors provides the reader with a neat package that relates welfare, laziness and criminality. As with the Romanow government, this logic applies just to kids and assumes that there is plenty of work if idle youth would simply choose to find jobs.

An article in the *Montreal Gazette* (July 18, 1993: C1), entitled "About 30 kids a year charged with murder," once again, illustrates the visceral images that are created by word connections, in this case, murder and poverty. The article begins by discussing that youth murder is a rare event, the writer acknowledging how the panic over youth murderers is exaggerated. It then proceeds to discuss several murders and the ensuing "lenient" sentences received under the *Young Offenders Act*. The subtle attack on poor kids comes at the end of the text in which a testimonial by a psychologist suggests that youth murders are so rare that it is difficult to make social or psychological generalizations about young murderers. This discussion is preceded by the ostensibly enlightened position: "If we really care about the poor kids, we should make sure they get the help they need when we send them to correctional facilities." Although the article attempts to be even-handed and progressive, by implication, it fuses youth murderers with poor children, a proposition that is entirely unsubstantiated. While the reader is encouraged to feel some understanding for young murderers, the text clearly generates revulsion and bewilderment and connects their "evil world" with poverty. The final testimonial in the article despairs that, "Most kids are subject to impulse, and that often results in something deadly." This alarming statement about the innately dangerous potential of youth (especially poor youth in the context of this article) is patently unsubstantiated, but it gains credibility because it is voiced by a consulting youth psychologist with a "Dr." in front of his name. This case is typical, then, of accounts that strive for credibility by drawing on the "expert" knowledge of highly placed, highly educated and by social definition, highly credible individuals.

In other cases, poverty, race and geographical location get mixed into the codes for badness. As part of a series of articles in the *Winnipeg Free Press* dealing with youth gangs (September 29, 1994: B1), one article presents detailed, graphic and seemingly factual police and court accounts of the nature and composition of gangs and their activities. But embedded within the text is a statement that frames the detailed accounts of gang-based crime. The statement asserts that the dangerous gangs are comprised of Aboriginal and racially mixed kids from poor and broken homes in the inner city, along with the admonition that, "with Manitoba leading the nation in child poverty, it's small wonder that the statistics also bear out in higher rates of crime." Like previous examples, the connection between poverty and crime (and also in this case race and geographical area) is made early, and it contextualizes the following descriptions in "culture of poverty" explanations that once again indict the poor, the inner city population and racial minorities for creating their own problems. As in most media accounts, social ills are reduced in the final analysis to the individual or the group. Such essentially biological or psychological determinist accounts are sweeping generalizations. At no time do these articles reveal that the subcultures they discuss are mostly law-abiding, that most violent and destructive youth crime is committed by only a few youths, and that despite all the disadvantages that a highly stratified society can impose on marginalized groups, these groups create vital communities that, in many instances, are obvious only because they come under society's closest scrutiny. While statements like the one in this article contain some truths, they are most damaging by omission in that they neglect to contextualize crime problems in a social structure in which people are given privilege on the bases of wealth, prestige, race and gender. The real problems that arise when profit takes primacy over individuals are hidden by the "panic about evil children." Overall, the articles on youth crime and its relationship to poverty illustrate just how pervasive and enveloping is the ideology against poverty.

The media rhetoric against the poor has changed somewhat in recent years, but the prejudicial referents against the poor and their associated familial and cultural practices are still present. And, most of the diatribes against lenient law-amd-order policy are infused with the discourse of "people unlike the norm." For example, a Globe and Mail article (October 17, 2005: A1), entitled "Street gangs and random violence: Winnipeg becomes murder capital," illustrates how a seemingly balanced article is infused with the rhetoric of class. The article focuses on the shooting of a seventeen-year-old youth in Winnipeg in October 2005. The problems of murder are described as problems of impoverished inner city areas, where crime is "commonplace." The article claims that the middle-class culture of Winnipeg is morally at odds with the city core, to the extent that "many people from middle class suburbs avoid entire neighbourhoods, even during the daytime." The article deliberately uses the language of class to separate the morality of the street from the morality of the suburbs: "Most of the victims of violent crime are aboriginals, Third World immigrants, gang members, homeless people or transients. Their deaths often pass without much notice." The article presents, unapologetically, a "rogues gallery" of anyone in Winnipeg who is not a "mainstream" citizen, including recent immigrants from the developing world. In a final testimonial to the immorality of the non-white, poor segments of the city, the article describes the victim as the son of "a well-known Winnipeg surgeon and a recent graduate of the up-market St. John's-Ravenscourt School. His death has sent a shiver of fear through Winnipeg's mostly white middle class." Apparently, the only citizens in Winnipeg who are distressed by the murder are middle-class white citizens. It is likely that reporters who engage in these so-called objective accounts of crime and anguish are not even aware of the racist, class-biased nature of their language. Being so much a part of the way we talk about crime, race and class, such stereotypical language is almost an essential component of public discourse. The report is overt in specifying the class characteristics of the victim and his family, juxtaposed against the speculated characteristics of the offenders, who live in Winnipeg's West End, which has "long been in thrall to a gang know as the Mad Cowz, made up mostly of young African immigrants, many in their teens."

A second example, taken from the *Vancouver Sun* on April 5, 2006, entitled "Vancouver millionaire's son abducted at gunpoint," describes a kidnapping by what bystanders described as "young Asians" (Bolan and Skelton 2006). The kidnapping resulted in the victim being returned, but the article is not only noteworthy in how it engages in speculation about the age and the race of the perpetrators, but also in how it distances the victim and the family from the social milieu of the ostensible offenders. The article makes a concerted effort to discuss the social attributes of the victim's family, including the fact that the kidnapping had shaken the city's "Southland neighbourhood of large country homes, pastures, and horse barns" and that the victim drove away from the "family's mansion… which is worth about $3.8 million." The article includes a series of comments by neighbours and friends that affirm that "these things don't happen around here," in the quiet, pastoral, wealthy community. The article distances the victim and his family from the underworld of crime, a distancing that places the moral world of conspicuous wealth against the implicitly immoral world of poor, ethnic minority young people. While the journalistic exposé is probably of prurient interest to the middle-class reader, it is an attack on the outsider, the "other."

It is instructive, here, to discuss the social construction of race and its association with the discourse of class and the definition of the "outsider." Critical race theory and post-colonial scholars have shown how race is socially constructed over time as a referent category for those who live outside the boundaries of good society. Race has an implicit reference to difference, especially with relation to moral conduct. The "other" in this paradigm is distinguished by a lack of values (both democratic and familial), by lack of achievement (mostly measured in monetary terms) and by lack of a personal or cultural legal framework (Hudson 2006). The linguistic practices of describing the "other" in racial and class-based terms "are necessary to the identity of western subject's idea of himself (Hudson 2006: 10). Clearly, in the articles described in this section, the press frames accounts of youth crime within a paradigm of "us versus them." And, this paradigm is framed around the penultimate moral citizen, who is white, well-heeled and influential.

Conclusion: The Denunciation of Race, Class and Gender

These examples of media discourse against the poor are different in several ways than are the invectives against single mothers and racial minorities. First, whereas articles against the latter categories are blatant and generic, the media discourse surrounding poverty is much more circumspect, laden with images of the poor as victims of economic circumstance, but all the while maintaining that the poor, as a generic culture, are volatile and potentially criminal. Second, the poor are treated in a more paternalistic manner than are women and racial minorities; generally, the sentiment is that the poor, while weak in both economy and spirit, need our help. For women and especially racial gangs, the sentiment is much more pointed and castigating, as if women and racial minorities are boldly and deliberately defying society's rules. Last, I would add as anecdotal evidence that articles dealing with youth crime and poverty rarely, if ever, use photographs depicting privation. For articles focusing on racialized and feminized crime, photographs of defiant minority gang members or snapshots of poorly dressed or overweight mothers are commonplace. The reason for the absence of pictorial descriptions of poverty may be that they are too representative of the stratified world of which the average citizen knows, and may lament, but chooses to ignore.

I have sought in this chapter to show how stereotypes against race, class and gender are embedded in news reports and that much of the information and the visual techniques that support stereotypical presentations lack journalistic integrity. Through techniques such as selective inclusion of facts, visual manipulation of messages, retraction of blatant inaccuracies and decontextualization of crime, the news media are distressingly consistent in the presentation of a burgeoning youth crime wave and in the condemnation of marginalized people. Even in their most objective moments, the written news media engage in fomenting public alarm over youth and are unreflective and unapologetic in their claims to journalistic integrity. They are the creators of young "folk devils."

CHAPTER 6

The Reality of Youth
Crime and Misconduct

I have entitled this chapter "The Reality of Youth Crime and Misconduct" partly as irony. I argue in this book that the presentations of crime that we encounter in the media and in political debates are not based on an empirical reality but instead are a deliberately constructed version of youth crime that serves political purposes. And, of course my version of the reality for youth could as easily be said to be mere interpretation. What is real, however, are the often unsubstantiated and/or inaccurate claims made by the media against youth. This chapter critiques those claims with a perspective that I believe is most closely aligned with and respectful of an adolescent's perspective.

I use empirical sources of information to illustrate three sociological levels of analysis: structural, cultural and personal. My macro-analysis is based on Canadian Centre for Justice Statistics data that looks at official rates of youth crime over time. Although these trends have been documented in critical works (Bell 2002; Alvi 2000; Schissel 1997), I discuss crime rate trends in the context of law reform and overall legal change. Further, I look at recent changes relative to changes in previous years to get some sense of how official crime rates fluctuate in relation to historical changes and occurrences

The second source of data is a survey completed in 2003/2004 with youth in open- and closed-custody programs in Saskatoon, Edmonton, St. John's and Mandan, North Dakota. The goal of this research was to understand the legal and social lives of marginalized youth, especially those in trouble with the law. These data give us some sense of the connection between relative privation, social neglect, criminal activity and legal disadvantage.

Last, I use information collected by Social Services, Province of Saskatchewan, on young offenders who had been formally processed by the legal system. This information is based on extensive interviews with the youth as well as supplementary material provided by schools, families and the courts. This wealth of information provides some sense of the personal reality of these "legalized" youth. The data, which are based on complex and detailed accounts and assessments of the personalities and lives of young offenders, illustrate that many youths who are continually in trouble with the law are victims at a most basic level and offenders only as a result of their personal, socio-economic and legal victimization. My analysis looks only at young offenders who have been involved in the sex trade. The fundamental premise of the analysis of these kids is that their problems are largely problems of health and not of criminality. One of the questions we need to ask ourselves is how problems of marginalized young people — which are primarily health related — get translated into problems of "crime." This last set of data is extremely important for this book in that it presents the complex reality of the lives of young people, only parts of which we see in ideological news accounts. And the parts that are presented by the media are constructed almost entirely around the criminal act and its legal consequences and rarely around the personal and social circumstances that bring youth into conflict with the law and the health problems that place them in extreme jeopardy.

Youth Crime Trends and the Politics of Crime Rates

As documented in earlier chapters, the misuse of official crime data that we see in news accounts about youth crime and the youth justice is common. The overwhelming sentiment is that youth crime rates are exploding and that the leniency of the youth justice system is responsible in part for this epidemic. If we accept statistics at first blush, as do most news producers, it would seem that there is reason for concern in light of the changes that have occurred in the last twenty years. Statistics, like most accounts of youth crime, are too often discussed out of context. They are presented in a social, economic and political vacuum, as if nothing is occurring in society except for kids doing bad things. News reports are abstracted, pseudo-empirical narratives, stories that present a fictional reality. As we attempt to contextualize national statistics and to deconstruct public rhetoric surrounding them, it becomes quite obvious that youth crime rates are produced by forces other than increasingly evil and dangerous youth.

Data taken from Statistics Canada and the Canadian Centre for Justice Statistics Uniform Crime Reports (UCR) are based on "actual incidents," which refers to crimes for which individuals are arrested. Of all the arrests made, only some proceed to the stage where a charge is laid. Consequently, some youths are not charged but dismissed, generally as a result of refusal of the victim to lay a charge, diversion strategies, or conciliation enforced by the police.

Figure 6.1 shows trends for all criminal code offences committed by all youth and for males and females. Most notable is the rapid increase in official crime rates that occurred after the implementation of the *Young Offenders Act* (YOA) in 1983. Much of the initial increase for all youth crime rates can be attributed to the inclusion of seventeen- and eighteen-year-olds in youth

Figure 6.1 Criminal Code Offences — Total, Male and Female Charges

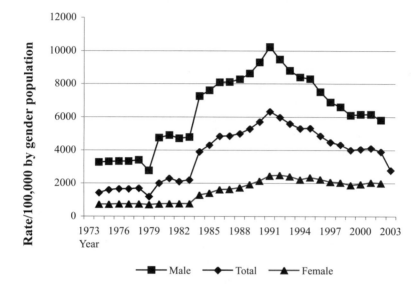

court as a result of the legislation. An interesting dimension of this state-produced increase is that it contradicts neo-conservative policy regarding less government as better government. In fact, the conservative, orthodox reaction to all crimes is, ironically, more state intervention. Despite the political contradictions involved in conservative law-amd-order policy, once the YOA had been in place for two years, the rate of increase slowed to 1991, when the rate began to decrease. This decrease is attributable to two phenomena: the decrease in overall crime rates (both adult and youth) in the developing world, especially Canada and the United States; and the overall decrease in charges for non-violent offences, which ironically accompanied an overall increase in charges for violent crimes by youth — based on the "get tough on crime" philosophy that was at that time driving more punitive amendments to the YOA. Since the peak period, from 1991 to 1993, total crime rates for young people have decreased up to the present.

As for the gender component, it is clear that, despite the public panic about increasingly dangerous girls, crime rates for girls have remained fairly constant over time. As with boys, the rates have gone down since 1993. The sudden drop in 2002–2003, especially for boys, is significant because it represents the influence of the new *Youth Criminal Justice Act*, which compels the police and other justice officials to divert kids from the justice system as much as possible.

These time trends are indicative of two main factors that contradict the public discourse about increasingly bad kids: youth crime rates have not increased progressively, and in fact, rates have diminished significantly, especially for males since 1991; and rapid fluctuations in crime rates are closely associated with changes in law, especially the implementation of the *Young Offenders Act* in 1984, amendments to the YOA from 1992 to 1998, and implementation of the *Youth Criminal Justice Act* in 2003. A commonsense assumption might be that violent crime rates were beginning to increase after the YOA and that the Act and ensuing amendments were responses to that criminal reality. If this were the case, however, the changes in rates would not likely coincide so directly with the implementation of the specific law reform. Furthermore, there is a mounting body of evidence that it was precisely the *Young Offenders Act* and the accompanying public fear of youth that translated, for example, into more aggressive policing, that were responsible for new violent crime rates. The reasoning is that acts of violence that were previously handled outside of the law — the typical schoolyard fight, for example — were being processed formally through the courts because people were more likely, than in the past, to report acts of youth aggression (Carrington 1995; Gartner and Doob 1994).

Figures 6.2 and 6.3 illustrate crime rate trends for crimes of violence and property crimes and give us a sense of how overall crime rates are affected by the seriousness or severity of the crime. Property crime categories include breaking and entering, motor vehicle theft, theft over and under $5000, possession of stolen goods and fraud. Crimes of violence include homicide, attempted murder, assaults, sexual assault and other sexual offences and robbery. The greatest decrease in crime rates for young offenders occurred for property offences and, as with overall offences depicted in Figure 6.1, we note that the decrease in rates for males is dramatic. For violent offences, the decrease in rates since 1995 is much less distinct; in fact, violent offences appear to remain relatively constant in the last eight years with some fluctuations, the most noticeable being that in 1999. In 1998, the Federal Youth Justice Strategy was implemented to deal with the perceived increase in youth crime in Canada. The ensuing political debates created a "mini-panic," which resulted in some "target hardening" by the youth justice system, especially for crimes of violence — hence the increase in violent crime rates from 1999 to 2001.

Figure 6.4 illustrates the ratio of young offenders to all offenders in Canada. I present this figure in light of a recurring theme in popular opinion and political discourse that young people especially are characterized by increasing criminality. The ratio has remained relatively constant over time with the exception of two time periods: 1983–1984, the period of the YOA, onward; and 2002, the period of the new Act, onward — both periods identified by law reform. It is clear that the legal changes are largely respon-

Figure 6.2 Violent Offences — Total Males and Females Charged

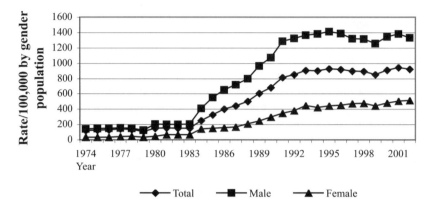

Figure 6.3 Property Offences — Total, Male and Female Charges

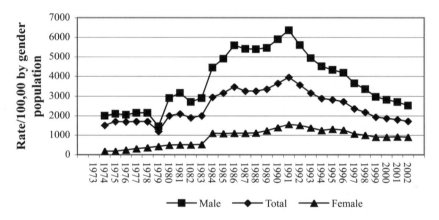

sible for the crime rate changes and not increases in actual youth crime.

The trends illustrate several phenomena that are rarely mentioned in public and political accounts of youth crime. That the *Young Offenders Act* drove up crime rates is irrefutable. The Act created a new orientation toward arrest and court processing that was more formalistic and I would argue, more punitive. There is no reason to assume that youth are more criminal than before, especially when we observe the declining youth crime rates in the last five years. When we place youth crime rates relative to adult rates, there is little evidence to support the contention that youth are progressively more dangerous. The major implicit conclusion from the adult-youth comparisons is that youths are being dealt with increasingly more harshly than adults. The *Youth Criminal Justice Act* was devoted in part to ensuring that young offenders would not be treated more harshly than adults; section

Figure 6.4 Ratio of Young Offenders to Adult Offenders

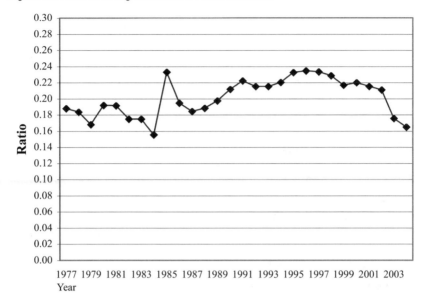

38(2) (a) states: "the sentence must not result in a punishment that is greater than the punishment that would be appropriate for an adult who has been convicted of the same offence committed in similar circumstances" (cited in Tustin and Lutes 2006: 64). This provision regarding sentencing, accountability and consistency with the criminal code is based, in part, on the justice system's much delayed realization that young people have been treated historically more harshly than adults. Specifically, under the *Young Offenders Act*, youth were incarcerated at higher rates than adults. In addition, 80 percent of custodial sentences were for non-violent offences and 33 percent of these were for breaches of administrative orders (Tustin and Lutes 2006; Bell 2002). Clearly, much of the increase in youth crime rates, which became the fuel for the public panic over increasingly delinquent youth, was the result of minor violations, including violations of court rulings and not the result of aggression-based threats to persons and property.

The new Act, which has welfare provisions for the treatment of children and youth as in need of care, requires sentencing/punishment for youth to be equal to adults but not less. We should expect that in a "child protection" atmosphere, the law to be relatively lenient with children and youth, and yet this is not the stated case. This is one instance, I believe, in which the "protection of society" framework of the *Youth Criminal Justice Act* overrides the commonsense, humanitarian principles that should apply to young people.

The Culture of Youth in Trouble: A Social Injury Perspective

I have used the words "social injury" in the heading to this section to illustrate how the identifiers of young offenders are largely about social injury (disadvantage and jeopardy) and not criminality. I have made this argument earlier, but what follows shows clearly that social-legal disadvantage is very much tied to social and personal jeopardy. The following discussion[1] gives us a sense of the social and personal lives of young offenders, and the social and personal disadvantage under which such young people live. What I describe below is representative, within the limits of probability theory, of young offenders in general.

The lives of young people in trouble with the law have two important aspects: the risk of offending is integrally tied up with education, victimization and drug use; and familial disadvantage and trauma have a severely negative impact on the welfare of young people. The race, wealth and gender of young people also have an impact on the nature and extent of risk. Familial disadvantage in the form of disrupted and damaged families can create individuals who are in relatively great jeopardy. In essence there is a subculture of marginalized and disadvantaged youth who live, at least part-time, in custody. I contend that they are not necessarily distinguished by their criminality, their socio-economic background or their appearance. They stand out because of the jeopardy in which they live, especially jeopardy associated with health, education and victimization.

Race, wealth and gender have a major impact on disadvantage and youth jeopardy. I argue in previous chapters that criminal/moral stigma have become associated with certain social groups through the discourse of crime news. The following analysis is intended to illustrate how such traits determine life chances. I show that youth who receive society's venom in the media receive the same type of censure in everyday life. There is a significant relationship between social inequality characteristics and indicators of jeopardy.[2]

The Context of Legal Involvement

Most young offenders do have a history of involvement with the legal system. Table 6-1 presents a rather telling story of young offenders: almost 15 percent of all the youth have been transferred to adult court at one time or another; almost 60 percent have lived in foster homes; 7.6 percent of the young offenders were ten or under when they committed their first crime and over 70 percent of these young offenders were convicted under the age of fourteen; and almost 50 percent declare their risk of re-offending as moderate or high. There are also some statistically significant disparities in legal involvement by gender, race and wealth. For example, males are questioned by police considerably more than females, as are poor youth relative to their wealthier counterparts. This is especially noticeable in the "more than five times questioned" category for both genders (23.6 percent of males compared to 8.3 percent of females) and wealth (17.9 percent for high income youth, 14.7 percent for medium income and 26.2 percent for low income).

As for crime conviction, males are convicted considerably more often than females, and this fact is most obvious in the "more than ten" convictions category. Interestingly, within categories of race, it appears that white young offenders have the greatest number of convictions, a finding that stands in contrast to the racial profile of young offenders facilities in western Canada and the U.S. In provinces such as Saskatchewan, Aboriginal youth

Table 6.1 Legal Involvement by Gender, Race and Wealth

		Gender		Race			Wealth			Total
						non-white				
		male	female	white	Aborig.	white	high	medium	low	
Ever Moved to Adult Court N=195	yes	**17.5**	**6.9**	13.0	10.7	58.3	**25.0**	**9.6**	**13.2**	14.4
	no	**82.5**	**93.1**	87.0	89.3	41.7	**75.0**	**90.4**	**86.8**	85.6
Ever Been in a Foster Home N=195	yes	39.7	49.2	33.9	43.0	54.4	**34.1**	**41.5**	**49.3**	42.6
	no	60.3	50.9	66.1	57.0	45.5	**65.9**	**58.5**	**50.7**	57.4
Times Questioned by Police N=175	none	**18.9**	**37.5**	**18.9**	**29.8**	**8.3**	**12.8**	**36.0**	**16.4**	24.0
	1 or 2	**29.9**	**33.3**	**26.4**	**34.0**	**16.7**	**28.2**	**29.3**	**34.4**	30.8
	3 to 5	**27.6**	**20.8**	**32.1**	**21.3**	**33.3**	**41.0**	**20.0**	**23.0**	25.7
	more than five	**23.6**	**8.3**	**22.6**	**14.9**	**41.7**	**17.9**	**14.7**	**26.2**	19.5
Conviction for (non-traffic) Crime N=173	none	**18.9**	**37.5**	**33.3**	**74.7**	**8.3**	46.2	64.0	54.2	56.6
	1 to 3	**29.9**	**33.3**	**29.4**	**16.8**	**75.0**	35.9	20.0	25.4	25.5
	4 to 10	**27.6**	**20.8**	**11.8**	**6.3**	**8.3**	10.3	8.0	8.5	8.2
	more than 10	**23.6**	**8.3**	**25.5**	**2.1**	**8.3**	7.7	8.0	11.9	9.7
Age of First Offence N=159	10 and under	**9.2**	**2.6**	7.5	6.4	0.0	65.9	81.4	62.0	7.6
	11 through 13	**66.4**	**56.4**	69.8	55.1	83.3	27.3	17.4	31.0	63.9
	14 and over	**24.4**	**41.0**	22.6	38.5	16.7	6.8	1.2	7.0	28.5
Risk of Reoffending N=190	low	50.7	61.1	**39.3**	**58.1**	**66.7**	**52.4**	**63.8**	**42.6**	53.7
	moderate	23.5	24.1	**28.6**	**23.8**	**0.0**	**28.6**	**18.8**	**26.5**	23.7
	high	25.7	14.8	**32.1**	**18.1**	**33.3**	**19.0**	**17.5**	**30.9**	22.7

Note: **Bold** indicates a chi-square test of significance of .05

are greatly overrepresented in facilities for young offenders: 76 percent of all young offenders in custody in Saskatchewan in 1999 were of Aboriginal ancestry. Moreover, Saskatchewan had the highest youth incarceration rate in Canada in 2004. We need to ask why non-Aboriginal offenders have the highest rates of crime commission and the lowest rates of incarceration. The Saskatchewan Commission on First Nations and Metis People and Justice Reform (Saskatchewan Justice 2004) highlights the over-incarceration of youth of Aboriginal ancestry as a fundamental reality in Canadian justice. It is interesting in this context that with respect to estimations of re-offending, non-Aboriginal youth consider themselves at a greater risk for re-offending than do Aboriginal youth. Embedded in these findings is the sense that Aboriginal youth are in custody for less serious offences than are their non-Aboriginal counterparts.

Context of Education

I argue in this book and elsewhere that educational failure is the primary conduit for young people to end up in the justice system; there is a high reciprocal rate between failure in school and experience within the criminal justice system. The risks are not only the social failure that often begins with school failure, but also the physical, psychological and emotional abuse and ostracism that failing young people experience. This important educational profile illustrates dramatically the absence of privilege and the presence of victimization of young offenders in the school system.

Overall, the performance in and attitude toward school for these relatively underprivileged youth was not a problem (see Table 6.2). In fact, as we peruse issues of performance, attitudes to school, and activity in school the results show a remarkably well-adjusted group of young people. The vast majority of youth express achievement levels that were average or above average (82.1 percent overall), as seen in "attitude to school" and "active in school." In both cases, the vast majority of students seem to have been well-disposed to being good school citizens. A majority (64.2 percent) of all students felt positively about school and 61.3 percent were active in school sometimes or a lot.

These findings stand in stark contrast to the variables that measure dimensions of trouble in school. For example, the majority of these youth had been suspended or expelled from school. Overall, 77.6 percent were expelled or suspended at least once and 42.8 percent were expelled or suspended five or more times. School expulsion is indicative of many things, but mostly that the young person and the school are not compatible. Continuing expulsion indicates clearly that the young person carries the stigma of being a school failure. It is interesting here as well that expulsion or suspension is related to both gender and race. Males are suspended considerably more than females, and Aboriginal youth are suspended less than their non-Aboriginal counterparts. In addition, the associated variable indicating trouble in school shows that this particular group of young people experienced inordinate trouble in school, to the extent that almost 60 percent of them got into trouble sometimes or a lot. As before, this phenomenon is stronger for males than females and for white and non-white compared to Aboriginal youth.

Although not as pervasive as being in trouble at school, there is evi-

Table 6.2 Educational Outcomes by Gender, Race and Wealth

		Gender		Race			Wealth			Total
		male	female	white	Aborig.	non-white	high	medium	low	
Performance in School N=201	below average	18.4	16.7	28.6	13.8	16.7	18.2	14.0	22.5	17.9
	average	63.8	66.7	57.1	69.8	58.3	59.1	73.3	57.7	64.7
	above average	17.7	16.7	14.3	16.4	25.0	22.7	12.8	19.7	17.4
Times Suspended or Expelled N=199	none	**15.6**	**38.3**	**17.9**	**26.7**	**16.7**	27.3	23.3	18.3	22.4
	1 to 4	**29.8**	**46.7**	**23.2**	**39.7**	**33.3**	34.1	34.9	35.2	34.8
	5 or more	**54.6**	**15.0**	**58.9**	**33.6**	**50.0**	38.6	41.9	46.5	42.8
Attitude to School N=198	negative	19.4	13.6	16.1	15.7	25.0	22.7	13.1	20.0	17.7
	neutral	20.1	13.6	23.2	16.5	25.0	22.7	15.5	18.6	18.2
	positive	60.5	72.9	60.7	67.8	50.0	54.5	71.4	61.4	64.2
Get into Trouble at School N=192	seldom	**36.6**	**56.9**	**31.5**	**50.0**	**33.3**	**43.2**	**48.8**	**35.3**	42.6
	sometimes	**28.4**	**24.1**	**24.1**	**26.8**	**25.0**	**25.0**	**31.3**	**23.5**	27.1
	a lot	**35.1**	**19.0**	**44.4**	**23.2**	**41.7**	**31.8**	**20.0**	**41.2**	30.3
Active in School N=194	seldom	38.1	40.0	43.6	36.3	58.3	31.8	42.0	39.1	38.7
	sometimes	23.1	31.7	27.3	25.7	16.7	25.0	23.5	29.0	25.8
	a lot	38.8	28.3	29.1	38.1	25.0	43.2	34.6	31.9	35.5
Afraid at School N=194	seldom	85.8	80.0	87.3	82.3	91.7	90.9	85.2	78.3	84.0
	sometimes	9.7	18.3	7.3	15.0	0.0	4.5	13.6	15.9	12.4
	a lot	4.5	1.7	5.5	2.7	8.3	4.5	1.2	5.8	3.6
Hurt at School N=191	seldom	81.8	81.4	80.8	84.1	66.7	79.1	81.0	84.1	80.6
	sometimes	13.6	11.9	15.4	10.6	25.0	11.6	16.5	10.1	13.1
	a lot	4.5	6.8	3.8	5.3	8.3	9.3	2.5	5.8	6.3
Bring Weapon to School N=192	seldom	**58.6**	**78.0**	67.9	68.1	50.0	**61.4**	**67.1**	**63.8**	73.4
	sometimes	**17.3**	**10.2**	13.2	13.3	8.3	**15.9**	**13.9**	**15.9**	15.1
	a lot	**24.1**	**11.9**	18.9	18.6	41.7	**22.7**	**19.0**	**20.3**	11.5

Note: **Bold** indicates a chi-square significance of .05

dence that these youth were also victimized and threatened at school. Sixteen percent were afraid "sometimes" or "a lot," and almost 20 percent were hurt at school at one time or another. It is also significant that over 15.1 percent of youth brought a weapon to school sometimes and 11.5 percent did so a lot. There is a sense that for a fairly substantial minority of these young people, school was not a safe place and that the school context appears to have been inhospitable for many of the young offenders in this study, despite their positive orientation to education itself.

The Context of Victimization

I extend this analysis of social victimization by looking at the actual threats to well-being that young offenders experience. Overall these young offenders certainly seem to be inordinate jeopardy. One of the arguments that I make in this book, and in my work in general, is that young offenders are *primarily* typified by threats to their health. The lives of the young offenders discussed here lend support to this contention. For example, over 25 percent of young offenders have thought seriously about suicide, and almost 30 percent have engaged in slashing or other forms of self-injury. While the overall rating of physical health would seem to be rather normal, issues associated with living on the street — physical assault, sexual assault, crime victimization, involvement in prostitution and gang activity — certainly suggest that their self-assessment of health stands in contrast to a relatively dangerous life. Over half the youth had been assaulted by a stranger, over 20 percent sexually assaulted and over 50 percent the victim of a crime. These indicators of an inordinately dangerous context are accompanied by the experiential reality that 11.2 percent of the young offenders had been involved in the sex trade, about 55 percent had been involved in gang activity and about 30 percent had lived on the street at one time or another. Certainly, the lived context for young offenders is one that few of us would wish for.

There are several noteworthy associations between the threats to well-being and race, class and gender although there are not as many as one might expect. The consistent lack of association suggests, in part, that the reality is similar for most young offenders. One of the main exceptions is gender based: in terms of sexual assault and involvement in the sex trade, girls suffer higher levels of sexual assault by strangers than do boys (45 percent and 10.3 percent, respectively) and girls are more often involved in the sex trade than boys (20.3 percent and 7.2 percent, respectively). In term of race, the only significant association is with gang affiliation: Aboriginal and non-white young offenders are more often involved in gangs than are their white counterparts. Wealth is related to the physical health rating and to having lived on the streets. Poorer kids tend to live on the streets more than their wealthier counterparts, and the former rate their health as poorer.

Table 6.3 Victimization and Threats to Well-being by Gender, Race and Wealth

		Gender		Race			Wealth			Total
		male	female	white	Aborig.	non-white	high	medium	low	
Thought Seriously Suicide N=192	seldom	76.1	69.0	77.8	74.1	58.3	75.0	81.3	64.7	74.0
	some	11.9	22.4	14.8	12.5	33.23	13.6	12.5	19.1	15.1
	a lot	11.9	8.6	7.4	13.4	8.23	11.34	6.3	16.2	10.9
Slashing or Self-Abuse N=200	none	73.0	66.7	71.4	72.4	58.23	**65.9**	**81.4**	**62.0**	71.5
	sometimes	22.7	28.3	23.2	23.3	33.23	**27.23**	**17.4**	**31.0**	24.5
	a lot	4.3	5.0	5.4	4.3	8.23	**6.8**	**1.2**	**7.0**	4.0
Physical Health Rating N=198	below average	10.1	11.7	7.1	11.3	12.5	**6.8**	**13.1**	**10.0**	**10.6**
	average	65.2	75.0	73.2	66.1	43.8	**56.8**	**73.8**	**68.6**	**68.2**
	above average	24.6	13.3	19.6	22.6	43.8	**36.4**	**13.1**	**21.4**	**21.12**
Physical Assault Stranger N=194	yes	51.5	48.3	47.3	53.1	63.6	59.5	41.0	56.5	50.5
	no	48.5	51.7	52.7	46.9	36.4	40.5	59.0	43.5	49.5
Sexual Assault Stranger N=196	yes	**10.3**	**45.0**	13.0	23.3	27.3	25.0	18.1	21.7	20.9
	no	**89.7**	**55.0**	87.0	76.7	72.7	75.0	81.9	78.3	79.1
Victim of a Crime in 2000 N=195	yes	51.1	60.3	60.0	49.1	63.6	56.8	49.4	57.4	53.8
	no	48.9	39.7	40.0	50.9	36.4	43.2	50.6	42.6	46.2
Involved in Sex Trade N=197	yes	**7.2**	**20.3**	5.4	15.2	8.3	13.6	10.6	10.3	11.2
	no	**92.8**	**79.7**	94.6	84.8	91.7	86.4	89.4	89.7	88.8
Gang Association N=197	none	42.4	48.3	**56.4**	**37.2**	**25.0**	48.8	40.0	46.4	44.2
	some	24.5	27.6	**29.1**	**24.8**	**41.7**	20.9	30.6	21.7	25.4
	most	33.1	24.1	**14.5**	**38.1**	**33.3**	30.2	29.4	31.9	30.5
Lived on the Streets N=200	none	68.6	75.0	75.0	69.8	58.3	**65.9**	**80.2**	**60.6**	70.5
	some	23.6	20.0	25.0	19.8	25.0	**29.5**	**12.8**	**29.6**	22.5
	a lot	7.9	5.0	0.0	10.3	16.7	**4.5**	**7.0**	**9.9**	7.0

Note: **Bold** indicates a chi-square significance of .05

Context of Substance Abuse

There are several myths about young people and drugs, especially with respect to illegal hard-drug use. The reality is that many young offenders use substances to their own detriment, many of which are not illegal substances. Significantly, and perhaps surprisingly given media hype about kids in trouble with the law, there is not a lot of hard-drug use. There are relatively high rates of cocaine use: almost 18 percent of the youth use cocaine

Table 6.4 Substance Use by Gender, Race and Wealth

		Gender		Race			Wealth			Total
		male	female	white	Aborig.	non-white	high	medium	low	
Cigarettes N=192	never	13.6	15.0	7.5	16.8	16.7	9.1	15.0	16.2	14.1
	experiment	12.1	13.3	15.1	12.4	8.3	22.7	11.3	7.4	12.5
	daily	74.2	71.7	77.4	70.8	75.0	68.2	73.8	76.5	73.4
Wine or Alcohol N=189	never	18.5	22.2	**13.0**	**23.9**	**25.0**	**33.3**	**16.5**	**14.7**	19.6
	up to 1 per month	23.0	29.6	**24.1**	**28.4**	**0.0**	**26.2**	**22.8**	**26.5**	24.8
	weekly	45.2	40.7	**51.9**	**39.4**	**50.0**	**28.6**	**45.6**	**51.5**	43.9
	daily	13.3	7.4	**11.1**	**8.3**	**25.0**	**11.9**	**15.2**	**7.4**	11.6
Marijuana N=191	never	**23.1**	**22.8**	15.1	25.9	25.0	20.9	29.1	17.4	23.0
	up to 1 per month	**9.7**	**19.3**	7.5	16.1	8.3	18.6	8.9	13.0	12.6
	weekly	**23.9**	**35.1**	22.6	28.6	16.7	30.2	25.3	27.5	27.3
	daily	**43.3**	**22.8**	54.7	29.5	50.0	30.2	36.7	42.0	37.2
Hashish N=188	never	48.5	60.7	45.3	52.3	58.3	61.9	50.5	47.8	52.1
	up to 1 per month	18.2	19.6	13.2	22.9	16.7	16.7	17.7	20.9	18.7
	weekly	20.5	12.5	24.5	15.6	8.3	9.5	22.8	17.9	18.1
	daily	12.9	7.1	17.0	9.2	16.7	11.9	8.9	13.4	11.2
Cocaine N=191	never	58.2	70.2	54.7	65.2	58.3	60.5	65.8	58.0	61.8
	up to 1 per month	22.4	15.8	24.5	17.9	8.3	18.6	17.7	24.6	20.4
	weekly	14.2	8.8	15.1	12.5	16.7	18.6	10.1	11.6	12.5
	daily	5.2	5.3	5.7	4.5	16.7	2.3	6.3	5.8	5.2
Heroin N=153	never	20.9	13.5	**32.1**	**15.7**	**8.3**	25.0	16.4	16.1	18.3
	up to 1 per month	79.2	86.5	**67.9**	**84.3**	**91.7**	75.0	83.6	83.9	81.7
	weekly	0.0	0.0	**0.0**	**0.0**	**0.0**	0.0	0.0	0.0	0.0
	daily	0.0	0.0	**0.0**	**0.0**	**0.0**	0.0	0.0	0.0	0.0
Uppers N=191	never	62.2	64.3	**48.1**	**71.2**	**58.3**	60.5	63.8	63.2	62.8
	up to 1 per month	11.1	14.3	**18.5**	**9.9**	**0.0**	14.0	12.5	10.3	12.1
	weekly	18.5	12.5	**22.2**	**11.7**	**25.0**	14.0	15.0	20.6	16.7
	daily	8.1	8.9	**11.1**	**7.2**	**16.7**	11.6	8.8	5.9	8.4
Downers N=187	never	67.2	75.0	**51.9**	**77.3**	**66.7**	67.4	74.4	65.2	69.5
	up to 1 per month	14.5	14.3	**21.12**	**12.7**	**0.0**	14.0	10.3	19.7	14.5
	weekly	15.3	5.4	**23.1**	**7.3**	**25.0**	14.0	11.5	12.1	12.3
	daily	3.1	5.4	**3.8**	**2.7**	**8.3**	4.7	3.8	3.0	3.7
Sniff Glue N=191	never	79.9	80.7	**75.5**	**83.9**	**75.0**	65.1	88.6	79.7	80.1
	up to 1 per month	14.2	14.0	**13.2**	**14.3**	**8.3**	25.6	7.6	14.5	14.2
	weekly	4.5	3.5	**9.4**	**0.9**	**8.3**	7.0	2.5	4.3	4.2
	daily	1.5	1.8	**1.9**	**0.9**	**8.3**	2.3	1.3	1.4	1.6
Sniff Gas N=189	never	75.2	87.5	74.1	81.7	75.0	69.8	86.1	76.1	78.8
	up to 1 per month	18.0	8.9	14.8	15.6	8.3	20.9	8.9	19.4	15.3
	weekly	3.0	3.6	7.4	0.9	8.3	7.0	1.3	3.0	3.1
	daily	3.8	0.0	3.7	1.8	8.3	2.3	3.8	1.5	2.6
Psychedelics N=192	never	**46.7**	**64.9**	40.7	54.5	58.3	53.5	56.3	46.4	52.1
	up to 1 per month	**32.6**	**26.3**	40.7	27.7	16.7	27.9	28.8	34.8	30.7
	weekly	**16.23**	**7.0**	14.8	14.3	16.7	14.0	10.0	17.4	13.6
	daily	**4.4**	**1.8**	3.7	3.6	8.3	4.7	5.0	1.4	3.6

Note: **Bold** indicates a chi-square significance of .05

weekly. The same trend appears for psychedelics and uppers and downers, prescription drugs that end up on the street: about 15–20 percent of youth use these drugs weekly. What is more significant in these data is the high use of alcohol, tobacco and marijuana/hashish. Marijuana and hashish are relatively harmless substances and the high use of such substances would seem logical for marginalized youth, many of whom are trying to normalize very difficult existences. The rates of tobacco and alcohol use, however, are more disturbing, given that they are dangerous substances that are part of mainstream culture. Youth are chastised and arrested for drugs like marijuana and hashish when much of the danger to their health lies with substances that are deemed to be socially acceptable. Most smoke tobacco (73.6 percent). The rate of alcohol consumption daily is 11.6 percent. The vast majority are addicted smokers and a not insignificant minority are alcoholics. Given what we know about these substances, we need to note that the major health risks to young people are from legal substances. On this last point, it is also worth noting that, although only a small percentage of youth sniff glue and gas, the effect for such youth is immediate and permanent brain damage.

To the extent that this group of young offenders is representative, their lives are signified by several things that we need to keep in mind as we focus on issues of social justice for youth.

Legal Involvement
- Legal involvement begins generally at a very early age.
- Most young offenders have spent time in foster homes.
- Transfer to adult institutions is not a rarity.

Educational Experiences
- Young offenders generally have positive attitudes toward school.
- Expulsion or suspension is an ever-present reality for young offenders.
- Success in school is elusive for many young offenders.

Victimization
- Self-injury is relatively common amongst young offenders.
- Physical assault by strangers is a reality for young offenders.
- Sexual assault is common, especially for female offenders.
- Gang affiliation and living on the streets is a reality for many young offenders.

Substance Abuse
- Many of the substances that threaten the health of young offenders are

either socially acceptable and/or are produced by mainstream corporations and end-up on the street.

• The highest rates of illegal substance use are for marijuana and hashish, both relatively non-injurious substances — although they are substances for which youth may be criminalized.

Jeopardy and Family Life

The social context in which many young offenders exist for at least a part of their lives is fraught with difficulties — troubles that most of us could barely comprehend — in terms of the things that young people do and their experiences in their family environments. I do not intend here to indict families as negligent because there are all sorts of obstacles and threats to well-being that families suffer, especially families who live on the socio-economic margins of the society. It is unreasonable to assume that dispossessed families have the complete facilities to care for family members. Rather, what we see is that many young offenders start off with substantial disadvantage and that much of their legal involvement, educational success, victimization and substance abuse are related to the troubles that they suffer within their family lives.

Family Precursors to Legal Involvement

Family trauma, not surprisingly, is intimately connected with legal troubles for young people. This is clearly portrayed in Table 6.5, where there are a noticeably large number of statistically significant relationships. For example, all of the relationships between family trauma and "foster home" and "risk of re-offending" are significant. Youth who have been abused, kicked out of home and neglected by parents live in foster homes more than their less traumatized counterparts. Similarly, these highly traumatized youth have higher risks of re-offending than the less traumatized. "Conviction for crime" shows similar tendencies: high rates of legal involvement associated with high rates of family trauma. The most noticeable example of this is the relationship between "kicked out of parent's home" and "questioned by police," wherein 30.6 percent of young offenders who have been kicked out have been questioned by the police more than five times compared to 12.1 percent of those who have not. The same trends appear for conviction of a crime.

In other words, legal involvement is not only an issue of crime committed but in many ways, an issue of family disadvantage. Although the dynamics of how family trauma leads to legal involvement are complex, the reality is that it does. Even with a less obvious association like that between "parental neglect" and "transfer to adult court," the relationships are significant. For some reason, the trauma of family life translates into certain youth being transferred to the adult system, a potentially very dangerous outcome, knowing what we do about the dangers that young people face in adult prisons, including extremely high levels of physical and sexual assault (Schissel 2003; Schiraldi and Zeidenberg 1997).

It is clear that being arrested and the trauma of incarceration and punishment are directed, in part, at those who are disadvantaged by family life. In effect, we punish many young people for the disadvantages they are born into; ones over which they have almost no control.

Table 6.5 Legal Involvement by Family Trauma

		Hit by Parents			Family Abuse			Parental Neglect			Kicked out of parents' home		Total
		seldom	some	a lot	none	some	often	none	some	most	yes	no	
Moved to Adult Court N=195	yes	10.7	15.2	25.0	**10.9**	**15.7**	**35.3**	15.7	16.1	11.1	**13.0**	**14.9**	14.4
	no	89.3	84.78	75.0	**89.1**	**84.3**	**64.7**	84.3	83.9	88.9	**87.0**	**85.1**	85.6
Been in a Foster Home N=195	yes	**37.1**	**42.4**	**59.4**	**26.2**	**66.7**	**75.0**	**26.2**	**54.5**	**57.9**	**62.3**	**28.7**	42.6
	no	**62.9**	**57.6**	**40.6**	**73.78**	**33.3**	**25.0**	**73.8**	**45.5**	**42.1**	**37.7**	**71.3**	57.4
Age of First Offence N=159	10 & under	7.4	3.6	10.0	7.5	4.7	6.3	9.4	4.4	5.6	**9.9**	**4.8**	7.6
	11 to 13	60.0	71.4	71.0	63.8	69.8	62.5	62.5	62.2	61.1	**71.8**	**57.8**	63.9
	14 & over	32.6	25.0	20.0	28.8	25.6	31.3	28.1	33.3	33.3	**18.3**	**37.3**	28.5
Risk of Reoffending N=190	low	**59.8**	**41.9**	**45.5**	**62.2**	**46.9**	**29.4**	**60.5**	**40.4**	**36.8**	**41.6**	**61.5**	53.7
	moderate	**25.6**	**22.6**	**21.2**	**25.5**	**24.5**	**17.6**	**25.9**	**30.8**	**15.8**	**24.7**	**22.9**	23.7
	high	**14.5**	**35.5**	**33.3**	**12.2**	**28.6**	**52.9**	**13.6**	**28.8**	**47.4**	**33.8**	**15.6**	22.7
Times Questioned by Police N=175	none	23.9	26.7	20.0	26.1	21.3	12.5	26.7	20.4	23.5	**18.1**	**29.3**	24.0
	1 or 2	36.7	30.0	16.7	35.9	27.7	12.5	41.3	27.8	11.8	**20.8**	**37.4**	30.8
	3 to 5	25.7	23.3	30.0	22.8	23.4	31.3	14.7	29.6	35.3	**30.6**	**21.2**	25.7
	more than 5	13.8	20.0	33.3	15.12	27.7	43.8	17.3	22.2	29.4	**30.6**	**12.1**	19.5
Conviction for (non-traffic) Crime N=173	none	**62.6**	**46.7**	**41.9**	**63.0**	**54.3**	**25.0**	58.3	53.7	47.1	**44.4**	**66.3**	56.6
	1 to 3	**22.4**	**23.3**	**41.9**	**21.7**	**17.4**	**50.0**	22.2	31.5	11.8	**27.8**	**22.4**	25.5
	4 to 10	**6.5**	**20.0**	**6.5**	**7.6**	**15.2**	**6.3**	9.7	7.4	11.8	**15.3**	**4.1**	8.2
	more than 10	**8.4**	**10.0**	**9.7**	**7.6**	**13.0**	**18.8**	9.7	7.4	29.4	**12.5**	**7.1**	9.7

Note: **Bold** indicates a chi-square significance of .05

Family Precursors to Education

Although it may be intuitively obvious that failure in education is connected to family trauma, we need not only to see the connections in empirical form, but also to think through the moral and ethical reasoning behind placing

Table 6.6 Educational Outcomes by Family Trauma

		Hit by Parents			Family Abuse			Parental Neglect			Kicked out of parents' home		Total
		seldom	some	a lot	none	some	often	none	some	most	yes	no	
Performance in School N=201	below avg.	18.3	9.1	27.3	**14.2**	**19.2**	**35.3**	16.3	21.1	15.8	25.3	13.6	17.9
	avg.	66.7	727	51.5	**71.7**	**61.5**	**29.4**	67.4	61.4	57.9	59.5	67.8	64.7
	above avg.	15.1	18.2	21.2	**14.2**	**19.2**	**35.3**	16.3	17.5	26.3	15.2	18.6	17.4
Suspended or Expelled from School N=201	yes	78.6	87.9	84.8	80.2	84.6	88.2	**72.1**	**91.2**	**84.2**	**91.1**	**74.0**	81.6
	no	21.4	12.1	15.2	19.8	15.4	11.8	**27.9**	**8.8**	**15.8**	**8.9**	**25.4**	18..4
Times Suspended or Expelled N=199	none	27.0	12.1	18.2	26.4	15.4	17.6	**32.6**	**12.3**	**21.1**	**10.1**	**31.4**	22.4
	1 to 4	35.7	27.3	33.3	35.8	28.8	35.3	**30.2**	**36.8**	**21.1**	**31.6**	**35.6**	34.8
	5 or more	37.3	60.6	48.5	37.7	55.8	47.1	**37.2**	**50.9**	**57.9**	**58.2**	**33.1**	42.8
Attitude Towards School N=198	negative	**16.0**	**6.1**	**30.3**	13.3	25.0	18.8	12.8	15.8	10.5	23.1	14.5	17.7
	neutral	**16.0**	**21.2**	**21.2**	15.2	21.2	18.8	20.9	10.5	21.1	19.2	17.9	18.2
	positive	**68.0**	**72.7**	**48.5**	71.4	53.8	62.5	66.3	73.7	68.4	57.7	67.5	64.2
Get into Trouble at School N=192	seldom	**51.6**	**15.2**	**37.5**	**51.9**	**27.7**	**25.0**	**52.4**	**32.7**	**26.3**	**32.0**	**50.9**	42.6
	sometimes	**26.2**	**39.4**	**18.8**	**25.0**	**29.8**	**18.8**	**26.8**	**21.8**	**36.8**	**22.7**	**28.9**	27.1
	a lot	**22.2**	**45.5**	**43.8**	**23.1**	**42.6**	**56.3**	**20.8**	**45.5**	**36.8**	**45.3**	**20.2**	30.3
Active in School N=194	seldom	37.3	48.5	33.3	38.1	45.8	31.3	32.5	50.0	52.6	**43.4**	**36.5**	38.7
	sometimes	23.8	33.3	24.2	24.8	22.9	18.8	27.7	21.4	15.8	**31.6**	**20.9**	25.8
	a lot	38.9	18.2	42.4	37.1	31.3	50.0	39.8	28.6	31.6	**25.0**	**42.6**	35.5
Bring Weapon to School N=192	seldom	70.4	57.6	51.5	**75.0**	**57.4**	**37.5**	**74.4**	**65.5**	**47.4**	**52.0**	**74.6**	73.4
	sometimes	13.6	12.1	24.2	**10.6**	**17.0**	**18.8**	**7.3**	**23.6**	**10.5**	**16.0**	**13.2**	15.1
	a lot	16.0	30.3	24.2	**14.4**	**25.5**	**43.8**	**18.3**	**10.9**	**42.1**	**32.0**	**12.3**	11.5
Afraid at School N=194	seldom	**88.9**	**69.7**	**81.8**	**88.6**	**83.3**	**62.5**	86.7	80.4	73.7	82.9	85.2	84.0
	sometimes	**7.9**	**30.3**	**12.1**	**8.6**	**16.7**	**18.8**	9.6	19.6	15.8	10.5	13.0	12.4
	a lot	**3.2**	**0.0**	**6.1**	**2.9**	**0.0**	**18.8**	3.6	0.0	10.5	6.6	1.7	3.6
Hurt at School N=191	seldom	**88.8**	**68.8**	**69.7**	**87.4**	**79.2**	**53.3**	**89.0**	**75.9**	**68.4**	81.1	82.5	80.6
	sometimes	**8.0**	**25.0**	**21.2**	**9.7**	**14.6**	**26.7**	**7.3**	**22.2**	**15.8**	10.8	14.0	13.1
	a lot	**3.2**	**6.3**	**9.1**	**2.9**	**6.3**	**20.0**	**3.7**	**1.9**	**15.8**	8.1	3.5	6.3

Note: **Bold** indicates a chi-square significance of .05

blame for school failure. As I have stated before, school failure is a conduit to involvement in the youth justice system. The question that underpins our moral reasoning here is whether youth are "failures" or whether our system of education, in its fiscal and instrumental goals to produce "educated" kids for the least cost, is the failure. As we define success on the basis of sitting still in class and learning and regurgitating the three "Rs", are we forcing disadvantaged youth into further disadvantage? Being suspended or expelled from school is clearly associated with parental neglect and being kicked out of a parental home. In an ideal world, we would expect that school would be the place in which kids recover from family trauma. This clearly is not the case. A stark example of this is the relationship between family abuse and getting into trouble at school. Of the young offenders here who have been abused in their families, 56.3 percent get into trouble at school compared to 23.1 percent of those who are not abused. Similarly, 43.8 percent of the young people who are hit by their parents while growing up get into trouble compared to 22.2 percent of those who are not hit by their parents.

We see similar results for victimization in school. High levels of parental abuse and neglect lead to high levels of fear and being hurt in school. For example, 20 percent of the youth who are abused often are hurt in school compared to 2.9 percent of those who are not abused; 15.8 percent of kids who are neglected often are afraid a lot in school compared to 3.7 percent of those who report never being neglected. It is also interesting that high levels of family trauma lead to high levels of carrying a weapon to school. The disadvantage that young people experience in family life is clearly associated with disadvantage with respect to security in school. As I mentioned before, an ethical logic would indicate that the school should buffer the trauma of family for young people. This is not the case.

Family Precursors to Victimization

The disadvantage of family trauma for young offenders is illustrated by its direct connections to victimization. Some of the serious indicators of victimization are related to all the dimensions of family trauma. For issues of self-victimization, family trauma is related to thoughts of suicide and to slashing/self-abuse. For victimization by others, the likelihood of being physically assaulted by a stranger is much higher for youth with family problems than those without. A typical example here is the relationship between "hit by parents" and "physical assault by a stranger": 74.2 percent of young offenders who were hit by parents "a lot" are physically assaulted compared to 43.4 percent of those who are seldom hit by parents. The same large percentage differences occur for the other three family trauma variables here. Family trauma also leads to very high risk of sexual assault;

123

Table 6.7 Victimization and Threats by Family Trauma

		Hit by Parents			Family Abuse			Parental Neglect			Kicked out of parents' home		Total
		seldom	some	a lot	none	some	often	none	some	most	yes	no	
Thought Seriously About Suicide N=192	seldom	**84.1**	**60.6**	**50.0**	**81.7**	**61.7**	**43.8**	80.5	67.3	78.9	68.0	77.2	74.0
	some	9.5	**31.3**	**21.9**	**11.5**	**21.3**	**18.8**	12.2	18.2	10.5	16.0	14.9	15.1
	a lot	6.3	**9.1**	**28.1**	**6.7**	**17.0**	**37.5**	7.3	14.5	10.5	16.0	7.9	10.9
Slashing or Self-Abuse N=200	none	**78.5**	**63.6**	**54.5**	**80.2**	**59.6**	**41.2**	79.1	63.2	63.2	**64.6**	**76.3**	71.5
	sometimes	19.0	**24.2**	**39.4**	**17.0**	**34.6**	**47.1**	16.3	28.1	36.8	**26.6**	**22.0**	24.5
	a lot	2.4	**12.1**	**6.1**	**2.8**	**5.8**	**11.8**	4.7	8.8	0.0	**8.9**	**1.7**	4.0
Physical Health Rating N=198	below average	8.0	**9.1**	**21.2**	9.5	13.5	6.3	11.6	3.6	5.3	9.0	11.1	10.6
	average	68.8	**78.8**	**51.5**	73.3	67.3	62.5	68.6	73.2	73.7	67.9	68.4	68.2
	above average	23.2	**12.1**	**27.3**	17.1	19.2	31.3	19.8	23.2	21.1	23.1	20.5	21.2
Physically Assaulted by a Stranger N=194	yes	**43.4**	**57.6**	**74.2**	**41.0**	**60.8**	**88.2**	**38.8**	**56.6**	**84.2**	**65.4**	**40.5**	50.5
	no	**56.6**	**42.4**	**25.8**	**59.0**	**39.2**	**11.8**	**61.2**	**43.4**	**15.8**	**34.6**	**59.5**	49.5
Sexually Assaulted Outside of Home N=196	yes	17.7	21.2	32.3	**13.2**	**25.0**	**52.9**	**12.8**	**18.2**	**47.4**	**26.9**	**16.9**	20.9
	no	82.3	78.8	67.7	**86.8**	**75.0**	**47.1**	**87.2**	**81.8**	**52.6**	**73.1**	**83.1**	79.1
Victim of a Crime in 2000 N=195	yes	**45.5**	**68.8**	**71.9**	53.4	60.0	76.5	58.3	48.2	73.7	56.4	53.5	53.8
	no	**54.5**	**31.3**	**28.1**	46.6	40.0	23.5	41.7	51.8	26.3	43.6	46.5	46.2
Involved in Prostitution N=197	yes	7.3	**12.1**	**25.0**	**3.9**	**17.6**	**35.3**	7.1	10.7	15.8	13.0	10.3	11.2
	no	92.7	**87.9**	**75.0**	**96.1**	**82.4**	**64.7**	92.9	89.3	84.2	87.0	89.7	88.8
Gang Association N=197	none	45.0	53.1	31.3	**44.2**	**50.0**	**11.8**	42.9	48.2	36.8	33.8	50.9	44.2
	some	24.2	15.6	37.5	**24.0**	**22.0**	**47.1**	21.4	21.4	52.6	23.4	25.9	25.4
	a lot	30.6	31.3	31.3	**31.7**	**28.0**	**41.2**	35.7	30.4	10.5	42.9	23.3	30.5
Lived on the Streets N=200	none	80.2	54.5	45.5	**77.4**	**67.3**	**35.3**	74.4	68.4	52.6	**51.9**	**81.4**	70.5
	some	13.5	36.4	42.4	**16.0**	**25.0**	**58.8**	18.6	22.8	47.4	**38.0**	**12.7**	22.5
	a lot	6.3	9.1	12.1	**6.6**	**7.7**	**5.9**	7.0	8.8	0.0	**10.1**	**5.9**	7.0

Note: **Bold** indicates a chi-square significance of .05

52.9 percent of young offenders who are abused often by family have been sexually assaulted compared to 13.2 percent of those who have not been abused. In addition, family abuse is a risk factor for involvement in the sex trade and for association with gangs.

Clearly, the abuses and neglect that some youth experience within family life have a profound effect on their immediate well-being. Placing this conclusion in the context of our discussions on legal involvement and education, it is obvious that family trauma is associated with a reality in which the lives of some young people are severely jeopardized. In effect, the young offenders in this study are characterized primarily by their disadvantage. Somehow, this disadvantage gets translated into criminality. The questions we need to ask are how and why this occurs. Moral reasoning would certainly dictate that disadvantaged youth need care: that the basic requirement in their lives is psychical and physical health. Results such as these, which focus on the lives of young offenders, indicate profoundly that the societal focus is criminality and not health.

Family Precursors to Substance Abuse

The dangers associated with substance use are well-established, and as I mentioned earlier, many of the substances that pose a direct and serious health threat to young people are socially and/or medically acceptable, despite the public rhetoric that young people are primarily illegal drug users. As Table 6.8 shows, the relationship between family trauma and substance abuse are consistent: high levels of family trauma lead to high levels of substance use. This connection between substance use and family trauma is clear and must be, I contend, part of an attempt by traumatized youth to normalize an otherwise difficult existence. Importantly, the connection between trauma and substance use and abuse is not a matter of criminality. It most certainly is a public health issue that is about psychic illness and the human need for psychic peace. Unfortunately, through the criminalization of street drug use, many disadvantaged young people end up in the justice system for what is essentially self-medication. And, as I have mentioned, tobacco and alcohol are mainstream and socially-acceptable but extremely dangerous drugs, which are also highly profitable for powerful economic interests.

Table 6.8 Substance Use by Family Trauma

		Hit by Parents			Family Abuse			Parental Neglect			Kicked out of parents' home		Total
		seldom	some	a lot	none	some	often	none	some	most	yes	no	
Cigarettes or Cigars N=192	never	15.3	9.4	12.1	18.3	12.8	0.0	20.7	10.9	0.0	6.8	19.1	14.1
	experiment	14.5	9.4	9.1	14.4	12.8	6.3	14.6	9.1	15.8	12.2	13.0	12.5
	daily	70.2	81.3	78.8	67.3	74.5	93.8	64.6	80.0	84.2	81.1	67.8	73.4
Wine or Alcohol N=189	never	23.1	15.6	9.1	26.5	12.8	12.5	29.6	10.5	11.8	8.2	27.4	19.6
	up to 1 per month	28.1	15.6	24.2	23.5	17.0	31.3	17.3	29.8	35.3	30.1	21.2	24.8
	weekly	39.7	62.5	45.5	40.2	53.2	43.8	43.2	49.1	29.4	43.8	43.4	43.9
	daily	9.1	6.3	21.2	9.8	17.0	12.5	9.9	10.5	23.5	17.8	8.0	11.6
Marijuana N=191	never	22.8	18.2	28.1	25.5	25.0	12.5	32.9	12.3	17.6	13.5	29.8	23.0
	up to 1 per month	14.6	9.1	9.4	12.7	12.5	6.3	8.5	21.1	11.8	9.5	14.9	12.6
	weekly	28.5	27.3	25.0	31.4	20.8	18.8	24.4	33.3	11.8	25.7	27.2	27.3
	daily	34.1	45.5	37.5	30.4	41.7	62.5	34.1	33.3	58.8	51.4	28.1	37.2
Hashish N=188	never	54.1	56.3	40.6	58.4	44.7	26.7	66.7	38.2	27.8	40.3	60.2	52.1
	up to 1 per month	19.7	18.8	15.6	16.8	23.4	13.3	9.9	29.1	38.9	23.6	15.9	18.7
	weekly	18.0	15.6	21.9	15.8	23.4	20.0	14.8	23.6	11.1	20.8	15.9	18.1
	daily	8.2	9.4	21.9	8.9	8.5	40.0	8.6	9.1	22.2	15.3	8.0	11.2
Cocaine N=191	never	67.2	63.6	42.4	69.3	53.1	31.3	68.3	51.8	55.6	50.0	68.4	61.8
	up to 1 per month	17.2	24.2	30.3	20.8	20.4	31.3	18.3	26.8	16.7	18.9	21.9	20.4
	weekly	13.1	9.1	15.2	7.9	18.4	25.0	11.0	17.9	11.1	18.9	8.8	12.5
	daily	2.5	3.0	12.2	2.0	8.2	12.5	2.4	3.6	16.7	12.2	0.9	5.2
Heroin N=153	never	16.2	19.2	23.1	14.6	26.3	15.4	16.9	18.2	14.3	28.6	12.6	18.3
	up to 1 per month	83.8	80.8	76.9	85.4	73.7	84.6	83.1	81.8	85.7	71.4	87.4	81.7
	weekly	0.0	0.0	0.0	0.0	0.0	0.0	0.0	0.0	0.0	0.0	0.0	0.0
	daily	0.0	0.0	0.0	0.0	0.0	0.0	0.0	0.0	0.0	0.0	0.0	0.0
Uppers N=191	never	73.2	48.5	40.6	75.5	41.7	37.5	73.2	55.4	44.4	45.9	72.8	62.8
	up to 1 per month	6.5	21.2	25.0	6.9	25.0	18.8	8.1	12.5	27.8	17.6	8.8	12.1
	weekly	13.8	24.2	21.9	12.7	22.9	25.0	13.4	23.2	16.7	18.9	15.8	16.7
	daily	6.5	6.1	12.5	4.9	10.4	18.8	4.9	8.9	11.1	17.6	2.6	8.4
Downers N=187	never	79.2	54.5	50.0	81.0	46.8	53.3	79.3	63.0	56.3	52.8	79.5	69.5
	up to 1 per month	8.23	21.2	31.3	10.0	27.7	20.0	9.8	18.5	25.0	25.0	8.0	14.5
	weekly	10.0	21.2	12.5	7.0	21.3	13.3	9.8	16.7	6.3	16.7	9.8	12.3
	daily	2.5	3.0	6.3	2.0	4.3	13.3	1.2	1.9	12.5	5.6	2.7	3.7
Sniff Glue N=191	never	84.6	75.8	69.7	85.3	68.8	75.0	80.5	78.6	94.4	78.4	81.6	80.1
	up to 1 per month	11.4	18.2	21.2	12.7	25.0	6.3	17.1	16.1	0.0	10.8	16.7	14.2
	weekly	3.3	6.1	6.1	2.0	6.3	6.3	2.4	5.4	0.0	8.1	0.9	4.2
	daily	0.8	0.0	3.0	0.0	0.0	12.5	0.0	0.0	5.6	2.7	0.9	1.6

		Hit by Parents			Family Abuse			Parental Neglect			Kicked out of parents' home		Total
		seldom	some	a lot	none	some	often	none	some	most	yes	no	
Sniff Gas N=189	never	81.8	84.8	65.6	82.8	73.5	68.8	82.7	75.0	83.3	**76.7**	**80.5**	78.8
	up to 1 per month	14.9	9.1	25.0	14.1	20.4	12.5	14.8	19.6	11.1	**9.6**	**18.5**	15.3
	weekly	2.5	6.1	3.1	2.0	4.1	6.3	2.5	3.6	0.0	**6.8**	**0.9**	3.1
	daily	0.8	0.0	6.3	1.0	2.0	12.5	0.0	1.8	5.6	**6.8**	**0.0**	2.6
Psychedelics N=192	never	54.5	48.5	48.5	**60.8**	**38.8**	**31.3**	**62.2**	**35.1**	**50.0**	**36.0**	**61.4**	52.1
	up to 1 per month	31.7	39.4	21.2	**30.4**	**30.6**	**37.5**	**26.8**	**45.6**	**27.8**	**34.7**	**28.9**	30.7
	weekly	12.2	12.1	21.2	**6.9**	**26.5**	**18.8**	**9.8**	**15.8**	**16.7**	**21.3**	**8.8**	13.6
	daily	1.6	0.0	9.1	**2.0**	**4.1**	**12.5**	**1.2**	**3.5**	**5.6**	**8.0**	**0.9**	3.6

Note: **Bold** indicates a chi-square significance of .05

The Jeopardy for Young People Involved in the Sex Trade

This final section is important for several reasons. First, it illustrates the extreme jeopardy in which marginalized children and youth who become involved in the sex trade to survive live. In this regard, we must remember that the involvement of children and youth in the sex trade is not an issue of the market exchange of money for sexual favours. It is in reality an issue of pedophilia and sexual exploitation. In fact, describing the activity as prostitution masks the fundamental reality that we are discussing the activities of men who sexually abuse children. We must also remember that society, in part through the activities of the crime control and justice systems, persists in treating such children and youth as primarily criminal, when they should be treated as children and youth in need of protection from sexual predators. Second, this section shows clearly that the issues that the young people in this particular street culture face are not about their own criminality but about extreme threats to their physical and emotional health. And, this phenomenon raises a question I have posed several times throughout this book: how and why do we persist in treating issues that are primarily about individual and collective health as issues of criminality.

There are strong associations between a life in the sex trade and high-risk substance use, self-imposed threats to well-being, threats to physical health, and threats of physical and sexual victimization. Life in the sex trade is filled with dangers. These dangers illustrate starkly the claim that I have made throughout this book: that in many ways the young people that we condemn for their criminality are highly vulnerable, highly exploited children and youth who are, many times over, more victimized than victimizer. For example, it is clear from Figures 6.5 and 6.6 that substance use is

Figure 6.5 The Effects of Sex Trade on Substance Abuse

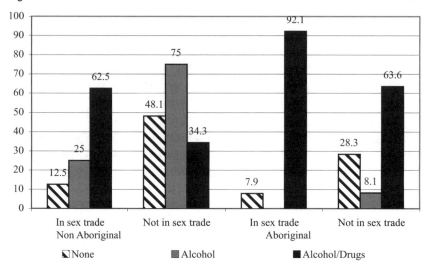

Figure 6.6 The Effects of Sex Trade on Severity of Alcohol Abuse

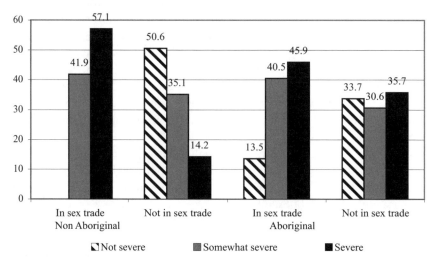

the norm for most young offenders accused of sex trade related "crimes." Moreover, youth involved in the sex trade are highly likely to use alcohol and drugs combined, compared to other young offenders, to the extent that 92.1 percent of all Aboriginal youth and 62.5 percent of non-Aboriginal youth involved in the sex trade are chronic drug and alcohol users. It is important to note that only a small percentage of youth in the sex trade do not use drugs or alcohol (12.5 percent non-Aboriginal and 7.9 percent Aboriginal). Clearly, emotional survival in the sex trade for youth is facilitated by using substances that mask the pain of the life and of course, simultaneously jeopardize the health of the youth.

The sex trade also engenders a great deal of self-damage. Figures 6.7, 6.8 and 6.9 all illustrate the extreme psychic jeopardy that the sex trade engenders. Youth involved in the sex trade have a higher likelihood of severe suicidal tendencies, have considerably more suicide attempts and experi-

Figure 6.7 The Effects of Sex Trade on Suicidal Tendencies

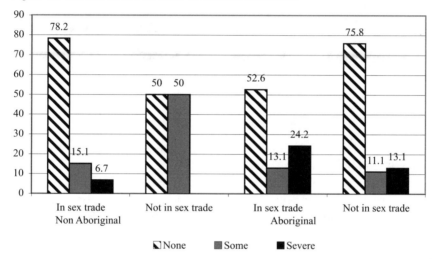

Figure 6.8 The Effects of Sex Trade on Suicide Attempts

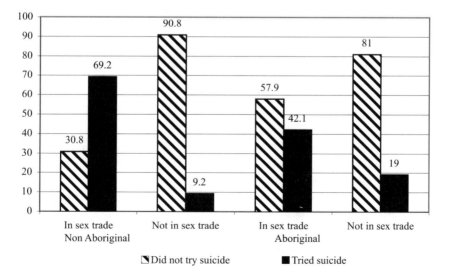

Figure 6.9 The Effects of Sex Trade on Self Abuse/Slashing

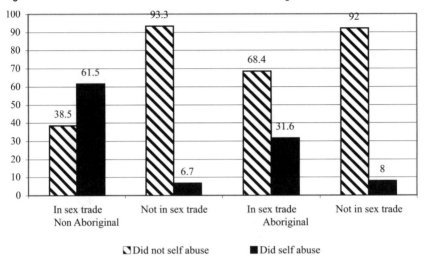

ence much higher levels of self abuse/slashing than do young offenders in general. The most telling results here involve suicide attempts and slashing: 69.2 percent of non-Aboriginal and 42.1 percent of Aboriginal kids in the sex trade have attempted suicide; and 61.5 percent of non-Aboriginal youth and 31.6 percent of Aboriginal youth in the sex trade have slashed themselves. Slashing has been studied primarily in the context of women in prison, where it has been found that the psychic damage of prison isolation, especially isolation from family, compels some women inmates to injure themselves in attempts to mask emotional pain (Boritch 2003; Shaw 2000). This research shows that youth involved in the sex trade engage in the same emotion-masking behaviour.

Similar results appear for teen pregnancy. The pregnancy issue needs some clarification. Unprotected sex is a valuable commodity in the sex trade and the highest profits are obtained from the prostitution of young girls who are willing to engage in unprotected sex. Simply put, one of the grim realities of prostitution is that johns will pay more for sex without the use of protective measures (Sachs 1994; Nyland 1995). The higher incidence of pregnancy of female youth prostitutes than other young offenders (see Figure 6.10) illustrates the relationship between life in the sex trade and exposure to the dangers of unprotected sex. [3]

Rates of teen pregnancy illustrate that non-Aboriginal youth involved in prostitution are being coerced or encouraged to engage in unsafe sex, or possibly, they are unaware or indifferent to the consequences of unsafe sexual practices. Such youth involved in the sex trade are much more likely to have been pregnant than their counterparts not involved in the sex trade

Figure 6.10 The Effects of Sex Trade on Teen Pregnancy

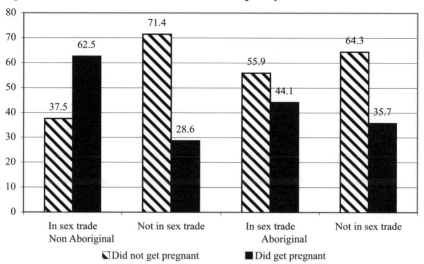

(62.5 percent compared to 28.6 percent). Interestingly, the relationship between prostitution and pregnancy for non-Aboriginal females is not as great as that for Aboriginal females; the percentages difference (44.1 versus 35.7) is quite small although still supportive of the argument that involvement in the sex trade exposes all youth to unprotected sex.

Involvement in prostitution places young people in a great deal of immediate physical jeopardy (with respect to physical and sexual assault). It is

Figure 6.11 The Effects of Sex Trade on Physical Assault (Outside the Home)

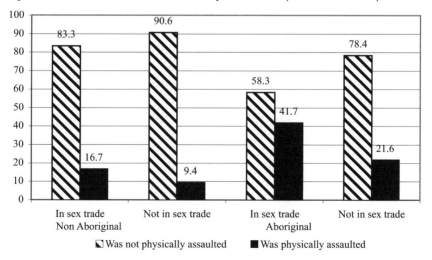

Figure 6.12 The Effects of Sex Trade on Sexual Assault (Outside of Home)

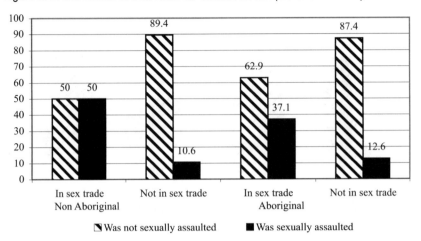

evident from Figure 6.11 that the likelihood of a young offender involved in the sex trade suffering physical abuse on the streets is high compared to youth not involved in the sex trade. For example, 41.7 percent of Aboriginal young offenders suffer physical assault if they are involved in the sex trade compared to 21.6 percent of other Aboriginal youth; the corresponding percentages for non-Aboriginal youth are 16.7 percent compared to 9.4 percent. The risk of physical assault on the streets is substantially higher for Aboriginal youth than for other young offenders.

On turning to sexual abuse outside of the home, the jeopardy for youth involved in the sex trade is considerable. For example, 50 percent of non-Aboriginal youth in the sex trade are sexually assaulted compared to 10.6 percent outside of the sex trade. For Aboriginal youth, the corresponding rates are 37.1 percent and 12.6 percent. In contrast to the finding on physical abuse, a greater proportion of non-Aboriginal youth involved in the sex trade suffer sexual assault than do their Aboriginal counterparts.

The pictures presented in this section on children and youth involved in the sex trade are fundamentally important because they force us to consider what we have done to kids who live on the margins. This highly disadvantaged, collectively wounded group of kids who are forced into the sex trade illustrates our social incompetence and apathy toward the neediest of our citizens. We need to consider that such children are not protected by the society, but are doubly jeopardized by the crime control system that puts them in jail and treats them like criminals when in reality they are highly dispossessed and highly aggrieved.

Conclusion: The Reality of Oppression

The empirical evidence provided in this chapter is an antidote to the hostile and damaging images about youth that we often see in public discourse. While empirical evidence is not always the best way to present a counter-discourse — especially given the critique of empiricism embedded in post-modern polemics, which highlights that statistics can be manipulated for polemical reasons — I use my research data on young offenders to give the reader a sense that the reality out there for marginalized youth is fraught with real, everyday hardship. I argue that this is not the hardship of criminality but the hardship of oppression, and it stands in stark contrast to the gun-toting, snarling images that we see in the media. The kids described in this chapter are children and youth whose lives are filled with troubles. And, as kids, they have very few resources for dealing with them, so it is not surprising that they end up in trouble with the law. All of this makes a law-and-order, punitive response wrong headed and immoral.

The findings for the young offenders in custodial institutions show their inordinate vulnerability to involvement with the law, which often begins at a very early age, their exposure to numerous foster homes and for some, incarceration in adult facilities. Their lives are further characterized by lack of success in school, despite generally positive attitudes to education, inordinate victimization including self-injury and physical and sexual assault, and exposure to dangerous substances. In essence, these are not the experiences of criminals; they are the traits of highly disadvantaged, highly vulnerable children and youth.

For children and youth involved in the sex trade, the dynamics are similar but more pronounced. Their lives are not lives of criminality but rather of extreme jeopardy. They are highly likely to face physical and sexual assault, self-injury, suicide attempts, sexually transmitted diseases, and alcohol and drug abuse. They are, at the same time, scrutinized very heavily by the crime control system, which persistently designates them as young offenders. The designation of such young people as criminals is unadulterated myth-making. They are, in fact, some of the most oppressed, most damaged individuals in society, and we not only turn a blind eye to their collective and personal dilemmas, but we criminalize them and brand them as "youth out of control." And, we embellish their conduct into an "epidemic of youth crime" that, as I have said throughout this book, advantages those who have the power to stand in judgment on marginalized people of all kinds. The reality is that youth crime is decreasing overall, that most young offenders are "in the system" for minor offences, and the reality of the lives of most young people on the margins is one of extreme threat to health and well-being and not one of criminality.

Notes

1. This discussion is based on survey research I conducted in 2003 and 2004 in custodial facilities and open-custody programs for young offenders in Saskatoon, Edmonton, St. John's and Mandan, North Dakota. The survey polled 202 youth on issues of socio-economic background, familial experiences and experiences with the legal system. The research was intended to understand the lives of North American youth who are highly marginalized and disaffiliated and who end up in the justice system.

2. An important caveat is that this is a relatively small data set so many of the relationships are non-significant although the percentage differences are large. This is a problem of small numbers within some cells of the tables. I ask the reader to take this into account.

3. The database does not contain measures of incidence of sexually transmitted diseases, and, therefore, this report is limited to using pregnancy as the sole indicator of high risk sexual activity.

CHAPTER 7

A Civil Rights Agenda
for Young People

The History of Youth and Political Nihilism

In this new millennium there is still a general malaise among the Canadian population in its attitudes toward young people. As Canadian society comes to grips with the neo-liberal transformation of global politics and economics, especially the paradox of productive efficiency and social justice, it appears that we scapegoat and blame children and youth for their sub-cultural deviance while simultaneously exploiting them as labourers and consumers. In the process, we absolve the socio-economic structure from blame for problems stemming from social inequality. Interestingly, the phenomenon of children-blaming is historically common. The following passage about life in a seventeenth-century English town echoes the alarmist rhetoric in contemporary Canadian media and political accounts about the inherent danger of children, their pathological vulnerability to alcohol, the importance of household discipline and "family values," the "problem" of poverty and the reluctance of youth to become involved in wage labour.

> A large proportion of Dorchester's population thus stood in great need of reformation and discipline. One segment of them caused special concern: those of the younger generation. Noisy adolescents are always alarming to their respectable elders. And at this time there were so many of them: the product of that "baby boom" generation born after 1600. Their families were sometimes too poor to support them, they often could not or would not enter covenanted service or apprenticeship and they were always in danger of slipping outside the system of household discipline, the very foundation of social order... even if they were not masterless, even if they were apprenticed to respectable trades, they were always liable to be riotous and undisciplined.... Their drinking was a particularly serious problem. The most dangerous kind of drinking involved young people, for in their case the authority of parents or masters was obviously at risk. (Underdown 1992: 79)

From the same source, the next description of an incident of youth deviance echoes the fear of the inner city that we hear in contemporary accounts of crime and victimization.

> London, everyone knew, was a sink of moral iniquity far beyond the imagination of pure-minded country folk. Be that as it may, the incident is further confirmation of the existence of a lively youth culture, a culture marked by frivolous jesting, a good deal of drinking and a keen adolescent interest in sex.... Apprentices being young people, their sexuality was a constant worry to their elders.... A paper was being passed around which Henry Follett, a dyer's apprentice, described as a catechism for women that could not hold their legs together. (Underdown 1992: 82–83)

Fears of urbanism, women's sexuality and volatile youth culture have long existed. It appears that youth crime was constructed rather typically during particular periods of economic upheaval and political uncertainty. As the reader will recall from Chapters 4, 5 and 6, much of the disorder attributed to youth today is believed to originate in the corruptions of poverty and womanhood. This last passage from Underdown's book reminds us of the first decade of the twenty-first century.

> Much of the disorder that plagued Dorchester was the result of the poverty that stalked it, as it did virtually all English towns. The realities of life for the majority of people in the seventeenth century should never be forgotten: the half-starved children, the women bringing up families in grinding, unending misery, the men demoralized and driven to drink or desertion by the hopelessness of it all.... The able-bodied poor ought surely to be disciplined and punished for their idleness, and their children brought up in greater godliness and better work habits.... The desperation of the poor during this bleak year is obvious from the sharp increase in the number of cases of theft of corn that were reported.... Many of these cases involved women worried about the welfare of their families. (Underdown 1992: 85–86)

Almost four hundred years later, we continue to blame able-bodied, single mothers on welfare for the corruption and the lack of discipline of their children, and ultimately, as Dorchester society did in the seventeenth century, we blame children for idleness, for being "on the street." I present this mirror of history not to suggest that child-blaming is natural or common or justifiable. On the contrary, this replay of history shows us how socio-economic systems that have discarded certain groups of people have commonly found moral scapegoats. Social-policy answers always revolve around the morality of the individual and never involve a critique of the nature of the economic system or the social order. We do in contemporary society what other societies have done in the past: we find it easy and convenient to blame children *qua* children for the ills of the world.

As we continue to blame children, we are confronted by a nagging contradiction, to which Postman (1994) alludes in his landmark work, *The Disappearance of Childhood*. In this study of the contemporary dissolution of the distinctions between children and adults, Postman argues persuasively that the television age has forced children to confront the world of adults, with all the horrific and inexplicable circumstances that entails. He documents how the modern mass media have made it impossible for children to be isolated from the adult world and how the entertainment industry has tapped into this reality by fusing adult entertainment and the language of the adult with that of the child. Postman's compelling argument forces us to confront the paradox and the injustice that, while we have abandoned childhood as a time of innocence and security, as our analysis of the news indicates, we preserve the category of childhood for treacherous, ideological purposes. Children are the modern prototypical scapegoats, forced to live in an adult world without the abilities to influence that world or defend their rights within that world.

As the ability of the state to provide for its citizens diminishes, the welfare and the civil liberties of the most vulnerable citizens become eroded. Canadian youth are among the most marginalized in Canadian society with respect to civil rights and conditions of life. This marginalization is increasingly, and arguably, the result of governmental policy that promotes business group interests at the expense of social programs and ultimately at the expense of youth, and that gives over to business the implicit right to set the social agenda (Bourdieu 1998; Giroux 2003b). Males (2000) has argued that the baby boom generation is protecting its financial legacy by ensuring that social programs that support young people do not drain the collective resources of a powerful, retiring generation. I argue, in addition, that young people bolster the economy to their own detriment because they provide cheap, unsecured labour and a fertile consumer market. This happens relatively easily, in part because youth, through their exclusion from participation in political processes, have no legitimate means of voicing concerns or influencing policy formulation in areas that directly affect both their life choices and their opportunities for success (Giroux 2003a; Schissel 1997). Youth are rather easy to ignore, and their civil rights to safety and security are essentially off the radar screen of human rights discourse.

The general dispossession of youth is accompanied by popular discourse that demonizes kids as dangerous. As I have shown, individual and corporate business interests, through their control of the media, offer portraits of young people as potentially dangerous, violent and morally bereft (see also Giroux 2003a; Glassner 1999; Schissel 1997). If the general public views youth as dangerous and prone to criminality, it is less likely to be sympathetic to the increasingly dire economic situation that today's youth face. This economic situation is the direct result of cuts to social programs implemented by the federal government at the insistence of business groups who have successfully lobbied against welfare liberalism (see McBride 2005; Carroll 2004; Teeple 2000; Burman 1996). Further, in marginalizing youth, the state undercuts social programs that target youth in particular. The relationship between poverty levels and youth crime is rarely discussed in media representations of young criminals. Instead, media images are of youth who are lazy, unwilling to work and criminally volatile.

To contextualize the marginalization of youth in contemporary society, I wish to illustrate the place of children and youth in the political economy by describing the nature of child and youth labour with respect to the traditional labour marker and with respect to military involvement. I deliberately call the state of children and youth in the new millennium world postmodern slavery — indentured labour that is so subtle in form and content that it appears to be empowering and liberating, neither of which is true.

Marginalizing Young People: Global Slavery

One of the difficulties in attempting to understand the place of children and youth in the modern world is that we really do not have a sense of where young people fit in the continuum between work and play. Common sense and research evidence suggest that children and adolescents need to grow and develop in a protected world in which they can learn from their mistakes. Social convention suggests that young people are not to be exploited in any way and yet they should be involved in civic participation as a training ground for citizenship. Childhood and adolescence, then, are times for enjoyment, freedom from responsibility, and freedom from mental and physical trauma. We assume that "carefree" adolescence is developmentally a good thing.

The reality however is very different. In many global contexts, children and youth have little chance to develop without trauma. In the developing world, children and youth are exposed to war, sexual exploitation, disease and privation in unprecedented proportions. In the developed world, children and youth are similarly exposed to trauma, albeit in a more subtle fashion. They are exploited in the labour market, with little access to the human rights that accrue to adults; they are exploited by merchandising industries, which prey on the culture of youth; they are exploited in the sports arena, where fun is replaced by militaristic discipline in the guise of perfection and teamwork; they are exploited by the industry of medicine, in which "child" pathologies are a new breeding ground for medical research; and they are exploited in war, in which young people fight while older people sit back and watch. And, for children and youth globally, their exploitation occurs primarily in a political context in which they have virtually no input into what happens to them. It is relatively easy to make the argument that a portion of the population that does not have the opportunity to engage in civic and political participation (at more than a superficial level) and that is exploited by their labour and their consumption is essentially in slavery.

Young people today are virtually indentured labourers (Schlosser 2002; Males 2000), are involuntary soldiers (Bourke 2000; Grossman 1995; Cohn and Goodwin-Gill 1994), are guinea pigs for medical and pharmaceutical research (Breggin 2002, 2001; Diller 1998) and are the victims of human trafficking for sexual and commercial exploitation (Davidson 2005, Fedec 2003). Given all this, it makes one wonder how we have come to a point at which we claim that children and youth are our most valuable asset.

Several historical and contemporary realities for young people throw into question the idealized view of the "culture of adolescence." A particularly important one is the involvement of children and youth in a labour market that provides low wages and poor working conditions and that denies the rights and freedoms accorded to adults in the labour force. Another economic hardship, connected but not identical to the youth labour market, is the level of youth poverty. Finally, there is the rarely acknowledged phenomenon of youth participation in war. While there are many other indices of the socio-political position of young people, work, poverty and war clearly illustrate that young people as a group take on adult responsibilities without the concomitant adult authority.

Youth, Work and the Global Political Economy

Kids work everywhere. The International Labour Organization (2000) shows that the vast majority of cases of child labour are situated in the developing world, although this is not exclusively the case. In fact, there are 2.5 million children involved in child labour in the industrialized world. The ILO (2002) estimates that 3 percent of ten- to fourteen-year-old children in the developed world are economically active. As the ILO report on child labour suggested: "In the review of annual reports under the follow-up to the ILO Declaration for 2002, at least five governments of developed countries acknowledged the suspected existence of one or more of the worst forms of child labour" (2002: 21). In 1995 in England, over 50 percent of thirteen-to fifteen-year-olds were employed at some time, and the Joseph Rowntree Foundation estimated that two-thirds of all British children age fifteen and under had a part time job. In the United States, the National Longitudinal Study of Youth in 1997 showed that between 1994 and 1997, 57 percent of all youth surveyed held a job sometime at age fourteen; at age fifteen, the percentage increased to 63 percent. Interestingly, the average working four-teen- or fifteen-year-old in the United States worked at least half a year. In Canada, labour force participation between 1996 and 2004 for adolescents fluctuated between 52 and 64 percent (Usalcas 2005).

One of basic human rights in any progressive society is to be able to work in a safe a secure environment for adequate wages. These rights should accrue to everyone despite social characteristics. Although labour standards are often violated in democratic countries, most countries like Canada leg-islate protection for children from labour exploitation, especially given our knowledge of how industries have historically exploited children for profit and how children are being exploited throughout the world. Worldwide, despite the United Nations' Declaration on the Rights of the Child in 1989, 250 million children work long hours in hazardous conditions (Parker 1997). However, in most countries, adolescent labour, as opposed to child labour, is considered a normal part of the transition to adulthood. What is rarely acknowledged is that like child labour, youth workers are highly exploited, wages are generally low, benefits are non-existent and on-the-job injuries are common.

Youth unemployment is higher that adult unemployment in almost all countries that report labour statistics. An international study concluded that worldwide youth unemployment is at an all time high; half of the world's jobless are between the ages of fifteen and twenty-four, an age group that constitutes only 25 percent of the total world labour force. The situation is compounded by the fact that the employed young people are largely working poor, who work long hours but are unable to earn enough to lift themselves beyond the merest levels of poverty (ILO 2004). From a purely instrumental point of view: "we are wasting an important part of the energy and talent of the most educated youth generation the world has ever had — enlarg-ing the chances of young people to find and keep decent work is absolutely critical to achieving the UN millennium Development Goals" (ILO 2004, Director-General Juan Somavia). The rising rate of youth unemployment is compounded by the finding that youth unemployment is excessively affected by labour market lows: an increase of 1 percent in the adult unemployment rate is accompanied by an increase of 2 percent in the youth unemploy-ment rate in countries for which the ILO has data (O'Higgins 2001).

Young workers are more likely than their adult counterparts to be injured on the job, and their injuries are relatively serious (Hendricks and Layne 1999; Marquardt 1998; Dunn and Runyan 1993). Approximately 40 percent of all work-related injuries for youth occurred in the fast food preparation industry. Federal child labour regulations in the United States prohibit anyone less than sixteen years of age from cooking or baking, and yet one-third of all injuries to youth in 1992 occurred among fourteen- to fifteen-year-olds who were identified as cooks. By 2001, this percentage was considerably lower, at approximately 15 percent (United States Department of Labour 2002). In Canada, the same sixteen-year age regulation applies to youth who work in the general construction industry, and yet in July of 1999, in Lashburn, Saskatchewan, a fifteen-year-old boy was killed when he was trapped between the cab and the box of a truck he was operating at a tire recycling plant. The boy was alone, unsupervised and obviously in charge of operating heavy equipment.

Many of the industries that employ youth as seasonal or "on-call" employees depend on exploited labour to maximize profit. The fast food industry, for example, is staffed largely by school-age employees, and the turnover rate is deliberately high (see, for example, Schlosser 2002; Reiter 1996). In contexts like this, employers rarely spend time and money training employees in workplace safety. It is expensive to do so and regarded as futile when the employee will only be on the job for a few months. Ironically, the types of injuries that occur amongst youth in the food service industry are "soft-tissue" injuries, and the Government of Ontario, for instance, is introducing legislation that would cut workers' compensation benefits for soft tissue injuries by deducting from the initial wage, the amount of work that the injured person could still perform while injured. As Doug Pearault, President of the Ottawa and District Injured Workers Group, argues, the most disadvantaged by this bill are young people, whose wages are already so low that the deduction from their assessment will leave no compensation (Bodnar 1999). Another indication of the exploitation of young workers is the difficult time they have protecting themselves. Attempts by young people to unionize fast food industries and retail mall outlets to secure their safety and labour rights have been consistently quashed (Schlosser 2002). Wal-Mart, the most prominent icon of successful global capital, has been accused and convicted of labour force violations against young workers, including making children younger than eighteen work through meal breaks, work very late and work during school hours. The company has also been indicted for demanding that young workers operate dangerous equipment, such as chain saws and trash compactors, in violation of labour standards in Canada and the United States. The sad reality is that this wealthiest of retail companies received fines on average of $100,000 for its crimes against children and youth, petty cash for this global corporation (Canadian Children's Rights Council 2005).

The rhetoric that accompanies youth work is often based on the presumption that illegal labour practices or poor working conditions and lack of workers' rights are just part of the learning experience. Because children and youth are unfamiliar with labour standards and are in many cases desperate for work, they are reluctant to protest unfair or unsafe working conditions and are, as a result, held captive by unscrupulous or negligent employers. They are hired because they do not know their rights or are loathe to demand them. Distressingly, little attention has been paid to the relative oppression that children and youth suffer in the labour market. The lack of concern for the rights of children and youth in the labour market likely arises from the belief that these jobs are transitory and will teach young people valuable work-related skills before they enter the adult workforce (e.g., punctuality, responsibility). The assumption is that these are not the types of jobs that young people will be doing as adults. However, many of these supposedly entry-level jobs are now becoming permanent for young people (Loughlin and Barling 1999).

To give this discussion a global perspective, there is an even more direct and menacing connection between western/global capital and child labour exploitation. In China, Thailand and other developing countries, children as young as seven work to produce toys and clothing to be enjoyed by children in the affluent world. Toy manufacturers like Disney, Hasbro and Mattel subcontract their work to countries in the developing world in search of cheap labour. While these companies deny direct involvement in child labour, they are complicit indirectly through subcontracting practices (Morris 1995). In Bangladesh, there are between 25,000 and 30,000 children working in garment factories, and the United States is Bangladesh's biggest apparel customer (Robbins 2005). Western developed countries maximize profit at the retailing level on the backs of children. To state it any other way is to mask the immorality with rhetoric of corporate responsibility to profit — to shareholders. The "morality" of capitalism takes precedence over the morality of caring for children. This fact is no more evident than in the reluctance of drafters and signatories to global trade agreements like NAFTA to include child labour protection. While there may not be the horrible sweatshops in Canada, the fact that we allow North American companies to exploit children in such ways says much about our real attitudes towards kids.

Young People and War

Military service has been and continues to be a place in which children and youth are indentured in extremely damaging occupations at the behest of adults. During the U.S. invasion of Iraq, George Bush stated several times that the young people of America are to be commended for their bravery and loyalty. Without apology, and in fact with bravado, the U.S. administration openly admitted that young people fight and die in wars, while, by implication, older, more powerful people sit back and command them to do so, and they offer the opportunity to young people as if it were a privilege. The legacy of war is tragic because those who are commanded to kill in many cases are young enough that they have not had the chance to develop the fortitude to withstand the trauma and guilt they experience. Ironically, it is youthfulness that makes adolescents such pliable soldiers. As Gwynne Dyer argues in his documentary *War*:

> It's easier if you catch them young. You can train older men to be soldiers; it's done in every major war. But you can never get them to believe that they like it, which is the major reason armies try to get their recruits before they are twenty. There are other reasons too, of course, like the physical fitness, lack of dependents, and economic dispensability of teenagers, that make armies prefer them, but the most important qualities teenagers bring to basic training are enthusiasm and naiveté. (quoted in Grossman 1995: 264)

Soldiers at all levels of the military bureaucracy know that young people are sacrificed at the altar of war. Gene Larocque, an Admiral during World War II, unburdens himself with the reality of his position as Rear Admiral during the Pacific campaign:

> I had been in thirteen battle engagements, had sunk a submarine, and was the first man ashore in the landing at Roi. In that four years, I thought, What a hell of a waste of a man's life. I lost a lot of friends. I had the task of telling my roommate's parents about our last days together. You lose limbs, sight, part of your life — for what? *Old men send young men to war*. Flags, banners, and patriotic sayings. (Terkel 1985: 191, his emphasis)

Politicians and military leaders most often frame military participation in terms of patriotism, character building and the preservation of democracy. These themes were important to the allied world in the two great wars of the twentieth century and were fundamental to the discourse surrounding the western world's involvement in international conflicts from the Viet Nam war to the invasion of Iraq. The presumption in the rhetoric of military conscription is that soldiers willingly agree to put their lives on the line for their country. Such voluntary military involvement is consistent with the principles of democracy and with the western ethos of individualism. The recruit is paraded within political and military circles as the cornerstone of the free world. The unspoken reality, however, of becoming a soldier is that the problem of employment is temporarily and sometimes permanently resolved. This instrumental economic reality is true for young people in general and more so for young people who live on the margins of the society.

That most soldiers, especially in the post-World War II era, are drawn from the ranks of the disadvantaged, is understandable when we consider that participation in war, is, in part, an artificially created solution for youth unemployment. As I argued in the previous section, young people are exploited in the labour market, they are a reserve army of labour to be drawn upon when required, and their employment is typically poorly paid and void of benefits. They are, in effect, a pool of exploitable labour without the political or democratic power to resist. Michael Moore's film *Fahrenheit 9/11* portrays scenes of marine recruiters promoting the armed forces to young, unemployed (or poorly employed) black men, pitching the forces as a place to get a pay cheque and job training. Simply put, the children of wealthy parents do not end up fighting wars because they do not have to. The children of poor, economically marginal parents fight wars because the military offers life chances, albeit largely temporary, that the economy cannot. Poor children and youth, as soldiers, are in effect indentured to the country and the fact that they are the most endangered by war is an unspoken and implicitly accepted reality. If the military is the best job youth can find, then those are the jobs they merit. Western meritocracy is a powerful ideological machine.

The two preceding sections help frame the theoretical argument surrounding "Blaming Children." There is a place for children and youth in the modern world but that place appears dark and foreboding. In fact, as I argue in this book, most institutions have elements of child and youth exploitation, as evidenced by the previous discussions on war and labour. If there truly is a hidden agenda to exploit children and youth worldwide, then our belief system and our ideological mechanisms must be geared toward legitimating exploitation. And, of course, more fundamental questions include who benefits from this exploitation, who uses their power to conduct a global attack on young people and what are the ideological mechanisms that educate us into a place of apathy and/or ignorance. For when we look at it clearly, it does not make moral or cultural sense to expose young people to the morality and morbidity of war while exempting older people. The concept of "blaming children," as part of the working ideology of the news industry, helps us understand how condemnation and exploitation occur together.

A Human Rights Agenda

This book has been devoted to countering the dominant ideology in Canada with regard to youth and youth behaviour, Demonstrating that there are child-protective and child-empowering orientations and policies that do work moves us beyond critique to a partial vision for the future. Unfortunately, academics and other "experts" have a tendency to get into a mindset that nothing works regarding crime prevention, and their negativity spills over to those who make and implement public policy. This pessimism is not only counterproductive but also dangerous in that it generates an apathy amongst public officials and youth workers that justifies ineptitude. As we have seen, this moral nihilism is fostered by sensationalist media, alarmist politicians searching for a constituency and fearful citizens. I am concerned, however, that one of the risks in advocating programs that deal with crime, deviance and dispossession is that we might be fostering more social control of already disenfranchised youth. This is possible if school programs, for example, become so intrusive into the personal and psychic lives of youth that they become violators of human rights. On the other hand, there is no escaping the reality that many children who are the foci of society's collective wrath are forced to live on the fringes of society. It is reasonable, I think, that part of the solution to dispossession is to empower the dispossessed both personally and politically. And the programs described in this chapter fulfil that mandate with minimal infringement on personal or collective rights. Because school is the context in which most young people spend the majority of their waking hours, it is reasonable to expect that most of the policies that attempt to change the fundamental human rights of children and youth should be connected to education.

But youth courts must not be forgotten as sites that need our collective attention if we are to claim to be a just society. As an instrument of social justice, however, youth courts face several problems. First, the courts are overburdened with cases. When youth are sentenced to detention of one kind or another, a further and associated problem becomes apparent: most closed-custody institutions are overfull. Second, even if the courts had adequate resources, their mandate is not activist; they are mostly unable or unwilling to address issues of poor health and social inequality (Green and Healy 2003). Third, the majority of youth plead guilty and are, therefore, merely processed in and out of the system. This is exacerbated by the fact that youth are not always represented by council and when they are represented by legal aid or court-appointed counsel, they are given very little legal time and they rarely have their cases contested (Schissel 2003). Given these concerns, effective alternatives to incarceration-based justice are needed. These alternatives need to be connected to a holistic notion of health that incorporates education, health and justice under one umbrella.

A community health-oriented approach to youth justice does not preclude the justice system itself. In fact, it asks that policing and jurisprudence expand to incorporate issues of social justice, social and personal health, and preventative social reform. Alternative schools and programs for healing in conventional schools, in concert with the legal system, become places where high risk children and youth learn not only educational and occupational skills (and meaningful apprenticeship) but also the skills for meaningful citizenship.

The Roots of Healing

International Programs

There are programs outside of Canada, such as the New Zealand Family Court and the Massachusetts youth prison system closure, that provide models for change based on reacting to crime. These programs are certainly part of the solution. In *Last One Over the Wall*, Jerome Miller (1991), the former commissioner of the Massachusetts Department of Youth Services, describes how he closed down the state's reform schools for young offenders, beginning with maximum security young inmates in 1969. The alternatives offered were based on community care, specifically community homes for young offenders. Former carceral resources were devoted to community prevention programs, which provided improved education and work opportunities for underprivileged youth. After two decades, despite concerted political pressure to reopen youth prisons, Massachusetts locks up fewer teenagers than any other state, its recidivism rates have dropped dramatically, adult inmates who were alumni of the youth system have dropped in half, and in 1989, Massachusetts tried a total of twelve youth in adult court, compared to Florida, which tried over 4000 youths in adult court. All of this occurred with no increased risk to public safety. In fact, Massachusetts came to rank forty-sixth of fifty states in reported juvenile crime. This astounding testimonial to a rehabilitative, community-based welfare approach, especially for maximum security offenders, suffered financial constraints in the early 1990s and state officials continue to feel fiscal and political pressures to reopen youth jails. Never before has a grand social experiment illustrated how incarceration ultimately creates a more dangerous society, and yet political detractors are powerful and influential.

New Zealand also has created a community-based youth justice system that essentially abandons the concept of incarceration in favour of a healing model for youths. Called Family Group Conferencing, this restorative, Maori-based model of conflict resolution was legislated under the *Children, Young Persons and Their Families Act*, 1989. In response to a history of high incarceration rates (second only to the United States in number of people per capita imprisoned) and a disproportionately high number of Aboriginal New Zealanders in jails, the program diverts children and youth from the justice system by making family conferencing mandatory for youth when criminal charges are involved. In the family group conference, the young person is confronted by the people his actions have affected. This includes the victim(s), the offender's extended family and youth justice officials. The offender is confronted by the anger of the victim(s), the responsibilities of the court system and the disappointments and anger of her/his family members. The conference focuses on the needs of the victims and the need to have reparation made not only in financial terms but more importantly in emotional terms. The philosophy of this alternative to formal, rigid justice is that offenders are given the responsibility to make things right with the victim and their own extended family. In the decision phase, the family deliberates in private as to the course of action needed to repair the psychic and socio-economic damage, and in the vast majority of cases, the entire membership agrees on a restorative course of action, including financial reparation and a family-based plan to make sure the young person is held responsible and accountable while being nurtured in the family environment. Overall, the New Zealand model, which is based on traditional Maori cultural values, attempts to replace the punitive and retributive nature of orthodox justice with a model of restoration and healing that is based on the future and not on past transgressions. Although the New Zealand model has been criticized recently for its lack of funding and it non-adherence to Maori principles, the program has seen an amazing decline in youth custody cases in its first twenty years of operation. For example, between 1989 and 1995, the number of youth in carceral detention dropped by 80 percent, with no appreciable rise in detected juvenile crime.

Several other international examples are noteworthy for their following of a non-punitive, restorative approach to youth justice. Australia has adopted an approach very much like the New Zealand program incorporating Aboriginal values and using "talking circles" to vent anger and frustration and ultimately to reach a resolution. Japan as well has achieved success over a fifty-year period by employing a "communitarian" model of justice, which uses community control whenever possible to make certain that the offender is not ostracized from the community through incarceration or abandonment. And like Aboriginal models of justice, the Japanese system is based on values of caring, responsibility and kinship and has progressively decreased the crime rate in Japan over a long time period.

Canadian Alternatives

We need to look, however, no further than the boundaries of Canada for alternatives to the formal youth justice system. Mediation and alternative measures for young offenders, as originally mandated by the *Young Offenders Act* and now the *Youth Criminal Justice Act*, have been used as alternatives to youth courts. The John Howard Society has for years been involved in programs that stress keeping kids out of custody and giving them opportunities whereby they can make reparation and, at the same time, receive counselling to restore themselves. Healing and sentencing circles are common in Aboriginal communities in Canada and, especially in Northern communities, are replacing the system of circuit court law, which tended to "process" people with little concern for cultural and personal considerations.

For centuries, First Nations communities have dealt with anti-social behaviour through a community well-being approach that has melded the best interests of the community with the best interests of the offender. The simple, yet profound basis of this healing philosophy is that it is more appropriate and ultimately safer for the society to bring the offender back into the fold than to punish or remove them from the community. When we consider that the typical repeat young offender in Canadian society is one whose past is typified by abuse and punishment, it makes little moral or practical sense to continue this abuse and punishment with legal sanction. Furthermore, from a healing perspective, when someone violates the community or when someone is punished, the community suffers collectively. The goal, then, should be to reduce punishment and resultantly to reduce personal and collective victimization.

Unfortunately, healing is anathema to the Canadian justice system. Conventional law is based on authority, rank and obedience in the face of punishment. As is apparent in any study of youth at risk (or youth in contact with the law), it is this abjectly authoritarian system of unyielding obedience and punishment in family, education, religious, social services and court contexts that traumatize kids. For proof of this, one need only read any history of Aboriginal residential schools in Canada to understand how all of these contexts can not only destroy individuals but also cultures (Quewezance and Schissel 2003; Schissel and Wotherspoon 2003; York 1990). Furthermore, conventional justice does not work. As Judge Barry Stuart states,

> The state of our criminal justice system has been exposed in numerous studies. It is a mess, a very expensive mess — wasting scarce resources and tragically, needlessly wasting lives. No one, not vic-

tims, offenders, police officers Judges, not anyone working in justice can believe the justice system is just, is a "coordinated system," or is working to any measure of success in achieving its stated objectives! In many communities, evidence mounts to suggest a professional justice system not only fails to reduce crime, it contributes to the factors causing crime. (Stuart 1993: 283)

Aboriginal-Based Alternatives

Aboriginal leaders in this country have lobbied for communities to become involved in dealing with issues of deviant behaviour and justice. The essence of an Aboriginal healing model is to take issues of community welfare that have been appropriated by professionals and give them back to the community. Aboriginal healing assumes that everyone is victimized by crime, including the offender, and that healing ultimately creates a safer, less offending society than does punishment. It is important to note here as well that this same philosophy provides a framework for many successful alternative school systems (see following discussions).

Community sentencing circles are based on decisions made by community members, offenders and victims. The high degree of consensus is based on traditional beliefs that shift the focus from solutions to crime to causes of crime. There is a growing body of material that meticulously describes the philosophy and success of sentencing circles and restorative justice programs (Stuart 1993; Ross 1993; Huculak 1995; Hollow Water 1997; Wachtel 2003; Coates and Umbreit 2003; Morrison, Blood, et al. 2005), and I will not repeat these descriptions here except to state that, where they are practised in well-established communities, they are relatively successful and stand in stark contrast to the unsuccessful punitive justice system currently in vogue. With respect to youth, sentencing circles and restorative justice programs represent a first step in empowering children. While they are based on restoring balance and harmony to a community, they represent only the initial stage of what I believe is a new way of approaching youth, especially youth at risk. The problem is that they still involve punishment, in the form of banishment, reparation and rehabilitation in the conventional sense.

I argue that such noble initiatives, especially when applied to youth, must necessarily dispense with issues of guilt and reparation and focus on issues of human rights (including physical, psychological and social needs), privacy, mutual respect, optimism and the disappearance of authority/obedience. In effect, I am suggesting a system of youth justice similar to the system of community resolution that did exist in First Nations cultures in Canada before industrialization and that is beginning to be restored in response to centuries of privation and oppression. Joan Ryan (1995) has produced a concise, reflective and anthropologically sensitive account of Dene traditional justice. Her research, produced through the voices of the Dene people of Lac La Marte, NWT, is an optimistic reminder that there are alternative ways of dealing with community members who break the rules, which do not involve lingering guilt or punishment in the legalistic sense.

As I read accounts such as Ryan's, one thing becomes perfectly clear: effective restorative justice involves respect for individuals, the community and the physical environment. It is also obvious that in many youth courts in Canada, respect is absent, from both youth and legal officials, and the notion of community and environment is poorly conceived in decisions regarding youth justice.

The Roots of Empowerment

While effective and innovative, all the above examples are necessarily reactive in their approaches to young offenders. They are intended to heal "after the fact" of the violation. There are, however, several education-based programs for youth that are noteworthy for several reasons. They are simple and effective; they are profound in their egalitarianism and their wisdom and understanding toward disadvantaged and abused youth; and they are proactive, they reach out to the youths and the community to help personal and community healing. Also they are based on a model of education that is revolutionary in its opposition to standardized education and in its willingness to minimize the use of authority and discipline. And most importantly, like the values inherent in traditional First Nations restorative justice models, they are based on empowering youth through the ideals and practices of respect, community and the future.

Princess Alexandria School

One of the successful schools is described in the first edition of *Blaming Children*. Princess Alexandria School in Saskatoon is a community-based elementary school situated in one of the poorer areas of the city and characterized by a relatively high transient population. Both the school and the community deal with issues typical of communities that are relegated to the margins of society, including street crime, drug and alcohol abuse, family dysfunction, racism and discrimination, and over-policing. Many of the students are highly disadvantaged when they enter their school years.

Although I will not repeat the description of the school that was contained in *Blaming Children*, I will reiterate some of the human rights principles that are the framework of the school. First, in an atmosphere of healing, violence and punishment have no place. To this end, the staff has agreed upon a philosophy of no punishment. Instead they create an environment in which flexibility is the rule and not the exception and in which acting-out is countered with options for the student, including making reparation or spending time alone. Expulsion is rarely an option. The school administrators and teachers have decided not to transfer difficult problems outside the school, as is often the case in other school jurisdictions, where social services or the courts are called upon to intervene. What this entails from a staff perspective is a good deal of tolerance and reflection. The staff is prepared to accept verbal abuse from the kids, knowing full well that the abuse originates with traumatic life situations. They accept the axiom that children's abusive behaviour is not personal, originates outside the school context and cannot be corrected with formal, authoritarian sanction. Clearly, the staff at this school either self-selects or is hand-picked, and staff members are aware of the needs of children who require care and nurturing before the three R's.

Standardized education presents a problem because it does not fit with the distinctive needs of children who have not had the advantages that others have had. In response, the school provides a flexible curriculum that allows for multi-grade education in which the classrooms are homogeneous by age, not by educational level. The students are assessed on the basis of individual progress and the concepts of pass and fail are absent from the system of assessment. Problems get solved based on the time priority of the student and not the school. At a general level, the students are treated with the respect that adults, at least formally, are granted by society.

The implication of this human rights approach to children is that the school and community are aware that before children can be confronted with the rigours of school, they must have their physical needs met, including food, clothing, shelter and security, requirements that should be guaranteed to all members of society. To this end, the school, with the help of community volunteers, provides things like breakfast as part of the natural mandate of education. The school provides work opportunities for the older students, whereby they may shovel snow or mow grass so that they can buy their own clothes or feed family members, if need be. While this program is valuable in providing work opportunities for older children, more so it demonstrates the inherent goodness in children, despite the hatred and mistrust of children that we see in the media. The school makes every effort to place siblings in the same classes or at least to provide siblings with opportunities to see each other, given the importance of family and caring. Overall, the school is prepared to treat kids with the respect and tolerance they deserve, especially given their outstanding responsibility in the face of extreme adversity.

Won Ska Cultural School

In *The Legacy of School for Aboriginal People: Education, Oppression, and Emancipation* (Schissel and Wotherspoon 2003), Terry Wotherspoon and I describe Won Ska Cultural School in Prince Albert, Saskatchewan. Several years ago, I had the opportunity to visit Won Ska and talk to the students in focus groups and talking circles and with the principal and staff on a one-to-one basis. The thing that struck me the most about Won Ska was how it exemplified an alternative education program that responded to the needs of troubled youth by creating an egalitarian education context, characterized by a minimum of top-down authority. Won Ska School was developed by First Nations and Metis parents, community agency workers, teachers from other schools who had a vision for a new school and youth in response to a high dropout rate for Aboriginal students in the city.

Won Ska's human rights based approach is successful for several reasons. First, the school is based upon the transition from childhood and adolescence to adulthood as a fundamental priority. In this regard the school deals with issues like substance abuse and privation, issues that resulted in legal problems in the first place. Second, the school is administered in a democratic way, with students, essentially, having the final say in their educational development. The teacher, as mentor, is of profound importance. The mentoring process includes not only training and the transmission of knowledge, but also a mutual, idea-sharing context in which the mentor listens as much as speaks. Most students in this school have missed out on the basic, fundamental rights of young citizens: a concerned and patient audience; a physically and emotionally safe context in which to live; a place where what they say is as important as what they learn; a chance to influence their life circumstances; an opportunity to make explanation and reparation; and a chance to see and emulate responsible, caring adults (Schissel and Wotherspoon 2003).

The focus on adult role models and the notion of mentoring is worthy of a bit more discussion here. One of the things that seems to be missing from modern, factory-like education is apprenticeship. For Won Ska, adult role models are fundamentally important because it is

> through interaction with and emulation of caring adults that marginalized youth develop basic life skills which include the following abilities: to do the day to day tasks that facilitate living: to understand what constitutes responsible parenting and responsible intimacy; to overcome the frustration that lands them in trouble; and to learn to trust people in positions of authority. (Schissel and Wotherspoon 2003: 73)

The school takes the negative experiences that its students experienced on the street and uses them as reference points for developing healthy, non-offending lifestyles. By focusing on the future rather than past transgressions, the school eliminates the criminal labels that have followed many students almost their entire lives. It replaces labels of "risk, "offender" and "high needs" with language reflecting potential and personal development. The practice of focusing on the future is consistent with First Nations spirituality and healing, which sees getting rid of guilt and blame as fundamental to the development of the whole person.

In addition to a healing-based orientation, the school adopts a relatively non-authoritarian, consensus-building framework of administration: students decide on curriculum, marking, school social events and discipline/justice. In conventional schools, the aforementioned are imposed in a relatively dictatorial manner. The logic and morality of consensus-based administration is so simple that it is profound, especially in application to dispossessed youth, but for all young people. In a world in which youth are disenfranchised from all levels of politics, investing their lives with basic human rights is not only the moral thing to do but also the healthy thing to do. Won Ska School teaches students that despite the legal labels that follow them, their role in the school is fundamental to their own welfare and the collective welfare of the school. The result is that retention rates are high. In fact, in the focus group comments, most students express the wish to remain in school twenty-four hours a day.

The enduring problem for what is essentially an amazing success story is funding. Won Ska is constantly battling for adequate physical and financial resources to maintain a working school. Furthermore, the school is continually fighting for credibility with the school board and the community because of its deliberate attempts to create a different model: it does not use a standard curriculum; rather its programs are student-driven; it focuses on one-to-one learning/mentoring, which is expensive; it refuses to engage in debates with local authorities regarding criminal students or potentially dangerous students; and it allows students to stay in school for "as long as it takes." There are, in fact, students in school who are well into their twenties and who take much longer than the designated three or four years to complete high school. In the end, the things that make this school particularly valuable and important are the things that threaten its existence.

Minor Programs — Major Successes
In this last section I wish to do something rather unusual but important. I wish to discuss several minor programs — or at least what would be considered minor in the eyes of the justice system — that have major implications for healing, especially for marginalized kids. The first is a program at the

Maclaren Youth Correctional Facility, a 460-bed closed-custody facility in Oregon. The program, Project Pooch, is simple and yet profound in its healing capacity. The program has young offenders involved in an animal rescue program. It started with one dog and one young offender and grew into a rescue kennel on the facility that includes rescue, grooming and boarding. The young offenders are involved in all aspects of the rescue, including liaison with the local animal shelters, rehabilitation of the dogs, advertising for canine placement, finding homes for the animals and scrutinizing the adoptive owners. Essentially it is a cost-recovery business that pays the young people a wage, provides them with invaluable experience in business and caring, provides a valuable service to the community and provides a profound sense of accomplishment for the young people in custody. To date over a hundred dogs have been rescued and placed in caring homes, and over a hundred young men have participated in the program. The directors discuss the success of the program with respect to individual success stories: the first participant in the program is now a successful dog breeder and has received a "Youth Making a Difference Award" from the governor; several participants have made presentations to community groups and the legislature in Oregon; and some have gone on to college. The reality of young men in custody is that many have never had caring relationships in their lives and have never had the chance to be valuable. This program provides the opportunity for damaged young people to make a difference, to learn to care about animals as dispossessed as they themselves may be. This is part of a human rights program for young people.

The second program is in Kamsack, Saskatchewan, and is a community response initiated by three reserves within the Yorkton Tribal Council. Given the legacy of residential school for those reserves, the community experiences high crime rates amongst youth and a declining population, resulting from youth leaving what they consider a community without opportunity. The Kamsack Family Resource Centre created a multi-agency crime prevention committee, and after conducting a survey of youth needs in the community, it set up a series of programs, including workshops on race relations, a community gym and sharing circles for boys and girls. The sharing circles are fundamental to the community's sense of youth rights. The sharing circles are an opportunity for youth in trouble with the law to share feelings and fears without interruption and to hear and empathize with the feelings and fears of others. The project involves elders and other community members. Initially it included only First Nations youth, but it now involves some non-Native youth. The circles have become part of regular after-school programming in the area. Once again, the focus of the program is simple and yet profound. It provides marginalized youth with the opportunity to be heard and to hear others in an uninterrupted, egalitarian and safe context, another fundamental requirement of a human rights program for young people.

The last example, simple in its focus and yet powerful in its influence, is the Saskatoon Community Youth Arts Program (SCYAP), which provides an opportunity for disaffected and damaged young people to develop and use their artistic abilities. SCYAP was created by Darrell Lechman in 2001 to provide a place for at-risk kids to engage in creative arts, primarily painting. The program was initiated to channel the talents of graffiti artists into positive initiatives, including exhibitions in mainstream galleries. One of the first initiatives was a community beautification project that involved painting dumpsters throughout the city. SCYAP provides marginalized youth with the studio space and the training to develop their artistic abilities as a form of healing. Most of the youths in the program have been in trouble with the law and/or have lived on the streets, so their needs for caring and guidance are high. Since its inception, the program has sponsored art shows for the youth and has established a permanent gallery for their works in the Mendel Art Gallery in Saskatoon. Because the majority of the artists are of Aboriginal ancestry, the program has an Aboriginal Youth Arts Leader, who combines traditional art with teachings in history and spirituality. A work painted by one of the SCYAP youth, Kris Moffat, is featured on the cover of a criminology textbook sold across Canada (Schissel and Brooks 2003).

It is relatively easy to see why the program is successful and why it is important for the kids and the community. As with all fine programs, SCYAP draws on the talents of youth and does not focus on their liabilities or their histories. It provides marginalized youth the opportunity to help the community, as exemplified by their creating works of art on dumpsters, a clever response to the community's hysteria about graffiti, and to showcase their talents. The artistic talent that seems to be common among the SCYAP kids is ability that is not valued in the school system nearly as much as abilities in math and language. In many ways, this program is an antidote to the stigma of school failure that many of the young artists have suffered. The program also provides the youth with an opportunity to manage, in an entrepreneurial way, the products of their work. The program bridges the "gap of trust" between marginalized youth and the community. Community members see the art, they see the creators of the art, and the youth are present in a context in which both the artist and the consumer can talk. Interestingly, art exhibitions and the medium of painting itself are held in high regard by more privileged sectors of the society and present a forum for ordinary citizens to "gaze in awe."

Conclusion

The schools and programs described in this chapter are profound in their understanding of the need to nurture students, especially students who are disadvantaged. The young people involved are not numbers; they are gifted individuals whose uniqueness becomes the basis of development and healing. These programs illustrate that standardized, factory-like learning contexts are contradictory to the needs of the students. The reality is that dispossessed youth need resources to make decisions that help them address their troubles and help them survive, and they need a context in which they can express themselves and learn to value themselves and others. Punishment, as a corrective policy, cannot possibly do this.

When human rights based programs treat youth like citizens with collective and individual rights, the successes are inspiring. When I hear stories about an elementary school child who works after school to buy clothes and food for his siblings, or who, after spending a sleepless night traumatized by drunken partying and fighting by adults, gets breakfast for her siblings, makes their lunches and gets them and herself to school, albeit in a disoriented and anxious state; or who at the age of eleven turns a trick and shares her bounty with other children to buy things at the 7-11 (*Saskatoon Star Phoenix*, November 25, 1995: A1), or when I realize that young offenders in closed custody willingly and faithfully rescue and care for animals that adults have abandoned, I am both humbled and ashamed. I am humbled by the strength, kindness and benevolence of children, especially in dire circumstances; and I am ashamed to be part of a society that fails to provide for the families and the children who live on the margins, and mostly ashamed by the venomous adult public rhetoric surrounding youth, which is unfounded, false, political and patently hateful.

The solution to the media, public and political distortion and demonizing, as the examples in this chapter suggest, is to empower children. In that regard, the *Youth Criminal Justice Act* may be on the right philosophical track with respect to diverting young offenders from the formal justice system. The problem with the Act, however, is that it is framed around public safety when it should be framed around other things: the restoration of the human rights and civil liberties of youth, underwritten by adequate and consistent public spending on effective alternative programs. However, given the individual-rights orientation of law, the collective needs of youth are difficult to ensure. Further, given the fiscal conservatism of the times, adequate funding most certainly has not been realized. Good alternative schools and creative programs for young people, however, seem to find the resources they need to survive, and they use those resources to blend the individual and collective rights very well. Maybe the Charter of Rights and

Freedoms needs to formalize the collective rights of children and youth. This may, for example, redefine the public attack on children described in this book as a form of hate literature, unacceptable both legally and morally.

I end with an excerpt (reprinted with express permission of Kenneth Noskiye) from a newspaper as an example of what we could report about kids, but also as a final reminder that, in general, society is terribly mistaken in its attitudes and practices toward children.

Street Kids Gather in Search of Family Love
by Kenneth Noskiye

When I was 15, I lived on the streets of Edmonton in the area known as "The Drag." I don't know why they called it that. Maybe it was because people got dragged into the areas by the drugs and the so-called fast life, which usually meant a fast death.

I ran into a group of other young people who hung out in the same area. We became known as the "Boyle Street Kids."

The aboriginal kids usually came from the northern parts of Alberta and Saskatchewan. Most of the non-aboriginal kids were runaways.

It was a struggle to survive.

Getting food wasn't too much of a problem. We figured out pretty fast where the food kitchens were. Church groups, bless their hearts, would also come onto the streets with food and vitamins.

Some of us tried to find jobs but we were all too young to work. So, we turned to the only source of income we could find: running drugs for the pushers. They wouldn't let any of us sell drugs, probably scared we would take over their markets. We ran drugs from the seller to the buyer. Of course, this made it safer for the drug dealers.

We used to wait outside hotels as the dealer inside was making a deal. When the trade was made, the dealer would tell us and we would make the transfer.

The girls in our group would scout for a "mark." It's really amazing how many men—usually middle-aged and white—would come down to The Drag flashing all kinds of money. When a target was found, we would make plans to get his money.

Violent robbery was the last resort. What usually worked was to get the guy to think he was going to have sex with one of the young girls, add alcohol and drugs and the next thing you knew he was passed out, with no money, no watch, no ring, no vehicle. And—if they were nice enough and they fit—no clothes.

The girls, all around my age, were not allowed to work as prostitutes. This rule was enforced not by us, not by the law and not by the older prostitutes, but by the pimps.

I knew prostitutes who weren't scared of anything. They weren't scared of the police, the perverted johns or any other prostitute. But, the pimps sent chills up their spines.

The pimps allowed us to hang around because we attracted the johns.

We always had to be careful about the perverts who drove around and around the block like clockwork. Sometimes, they would pull over and ask one of us, usually a boy, to come with them. Any boy who went with a john was rarely seen afterward. Probably, he was too ashamed for what the john made him do.

The police were about our only friends. They used us to keep track of the johns, especially those who asked for kids.

We got to know the police on a first-name basis. One time, a cop picked us up, about 10 of us. We thought we were getting arrested. Instead, he took us to a football game. The Eskimos kicked ass that day. We cheered.

That was almost 20 years ago.

Today, when I hear stories about street kids, I am saddened. I hate hearing the streets glamorized, like it was some kind of "NYPD Blue" television show. It's kids trying to survive the only way they know how.

The worst part is when I hear people who think they know all the answers from the warmth of their homes blame the parents of street kids. Most of the kids don't even know where their parents are.

These people blame the police for not doing anything, when the police are sometimes the only people the kids turn to for help. They blame outreach workers, who work endlessly for the kids.

I get unsettled when I hear a politician say, "We have to get tough," knowing perfectly well politicians are sometimes a prostitute's best customers.

Just before I turned 16, I was walking by myself. It was raining. I stopped at a house and stood under a porch to escape the rain. I looked through the window.

I saw a family watching television, eating popcorn and having fun together. I stood there and wished not for a car, not for a million dollars, not for a mansion to live in. I wished I had a family, someone to care and love me.

I walked away, back into the rain, back to the only family I knew, the street kids!

All they're trying to do is survive.

Reprinted with express permission of Kenneth Noskiye.

Bibliography

Alvi, Shahid. 2000. *Youth and the Canadian Criminal Justice System*. Cincinnati, OH: Anderson.

Anderson, Margaret.1988. *Thinking about Women: Sociological Perspectives on Sex and Gender*. New York: MacMillan Publishing.

Balbus, Isaac.1973. *Dialectics of Repression*. New York: Russell Sage Foundations.

Basran, Gurcharn, Charan Gill and Brian MacLean. 1995. *Farmworkers and Their Children*. Vancouver: Collective Press.

Becker, Howard S. 1963. *Outsiders: Studies in the Sociology of Deviance*. New York: Free Press.

Bell, S.J. 2002. *Young Offenders and Juvenile Justice: A Century after the Fact* (Second ed.). Toronto: Thompson Nelson.

Bingol, N., C. Schuster, M. Fruchs, et al. 1987. "The Influence of Socio-economic Factors on the Occurrence of Fetal Alcohol Syndrome." *Advances in Alcohol and Substance Abuse* 6: 105–18.

Bodnar, Chris. 1999. "Students May Hurt from New Workers' Comp Bill." The Fulcrum Online. Available at <www.aix2.uottawa.ca/~fulcrum/58-04/news/Smhfnwcb.html> (accessed May 5, 2006).

Bolan, Kim, and Chad Skelton. 2006. "Vancouver Millionaire's Son Abducted at Gunpoint." Vancouver Sun, April 5, 2006. Available at <www.canada.com/nationalpost/news/story.html> (accessed May 3, 2006).

Boritch, Helen. 2003. "Women in Prison in Canada." In B. Schissel and C. Brooks.

Bourdieu, P. 1999. *The Weight of the World: Social Suffering in Contemporary Society*. Stanford: Stanford University Press.

Bourke, Joanna. 1999. *An Intimate History of Killing*. London. Granta.

Box, Steven. 1983. *Power, Crime, and Mystification*. New York: Tavistock.

_____. 1987. *Recession, Crime and Punishment*. Basingstoke, UK: Palgrave MacMillan.

Bradley, Ann. 1994. "A Morality Play for our Times." *Living Marxism* January: 10–13.

Breggin, Peter R. 2001. *Talking Back to Ritalin, Revised*. Cambridge, MA: Perseus.

_____. 2002. *The Ritalin Fact Book: What Your Doctor Won't Tell You*. Cambridge, MA: Perseus.

Brownlee, Jamie. 2005. *Ruling Canada: Corporate Cohesion and Democracy*. Halifax, NS: Fernwood.

Burman, P.1996. *Poverty's Bonds: Power and Agency in the Social Relations of Welfare*. Toronto: Thompson Educational Publishing.

Canadian Broadcasting Corporation. 2005. "Attack crystal meth now, N.D. politician says." *CBC News*, June 10. Available at <sask.cbc.ca/regional/> (accessed on October 23, 2005).

Canadian Children's Rights Council. 2005. "Protest Wal-Mart Child Labour." Available at <www.canadiancrc.com/articles/AFL-CIO_Protest_Wal-Mart_Child_labor_22JUL05> (accessed May 5, 2006).

Cantor, D., and K.C. Land. 1985. "Unemployment and Crime Rates in the Post-World War II United States: A Theoretical and Empirical Analysis." *American Sociological Review* (50): 317–32.

Carrigan, D.O. 1991. *Crime and Punishment in Canada: A History*. Toronto: McClelland and Stewart.

_____. 1998. *Juvenile Delinquency In Canada: A History*. Concord, ON: Irwin.

Carrington, P. 1995. "Has Violent Crime Increased? Comment on Corrado and Markwart." *Canadian Journal of Criminology* 37: 61–74.

Carroll, William. 2004. *Corporate Power in a Globalizing World: A Study in Elite Social Organization*. Don Mills, ON: Oxford University Press.

Cayley, David. 1998. *The Expanding Prison: The Crisis in Crime and Punishment and the Search for Alternatives*. Toronto: House of Anansi.

Chambliss, William. 1969. *Crime and the Legal Process*. New York: McGraw-Hill

Chomsky, Noam. 2002. *Hegemony or Survival? America's Quest for Global Dominance*. New York: Metropolitan.

Christie, Nils. 2000. *Crime Control as Industry: Toward Gulags, Western Style*. New York: Routledge.

Coates, R.B., M. Umbreit, and B. Vos. 2003. "Restorative Justice Circles: An Exploratory Study." *Contemporary Justice Review*, 6, 3: 265–78.

Cohen, Stanley. 1980 *Folk Devils and Moral Panics: The Creation of the Mods and Rockers*. New York: St. Martin's.

_____. 1985. *Visions of Social Control*. Toronto: Polity.

Cohn, Ilene, and Gus Goodwin-Gill. 1994. *Child Soldiers: The Role of Children in Armed Conflict*. Oxford: Clarendon.

Collier, R. 1998. *Masculinities, Crime and Criminology: Men, Corporeality and the Criminal(ised) Body* London: Sage.

Comack, Elizabeth. 1991. "We will get some good out of this riot yet: The Canadian State, Drug Legislation and Class Conflict." In Elizabeth Comack and Stephen Brickey (eds.), *The Social Basis of Law: Critical Readings in the Sociology of Law*. Toronto: Garamond.

Currie, Dawn. 1991. "Realist Criminology, Women and Social Transformation in Canada." In Brian MacLean and Dragan Milovanovic (eds.), *New Directions in Critical Criminology*. Vancouver: Collective Press.

Currie, E. 1986. "The Transformation of Juvenile Justice in Canada." In B.D. MacLean (ed.), *The Political Economy of Crime*. Scarborough, ON: Prentice Hall.

Daniels, Cynthia. 1998. *Lost Fathers: The Politics of Fatherlessness in America*. New York: St. Martin's Griffin.

Davidson, Julia O'Connell. 2005. *Children in the Global Sex Trade*. Cambridge, MA: Polity Press.

Department of Justice Canada. 1999. *Youth Criminal Justice Act: Backgrounder*. Ottawa: Government of Canada

_____. 1999. *A Strategy for the Renewal of Youth Justice*. Ottawa: Department of Justice.

Diller, Lawrence H. 1998. *Running on Ritalin: A Physician Reflects on Children, Society, and Performance in a Pill*. New York: Bantam.

Earls, C.P., and H. David. 1990. "Early Family Sexual Experiences of Male and

Female Prostitutes." *Canada's Mental Health* December: 7–11.

Edelman, Bernard. 1985. *Dear America: Letters Home from Viet Nam*. New York: W.W. Norton.

Elliot, D.S., and S. Ageton. 1980. "Reconciling Race and Class Differences in Self-Reported and Official Estimates of Delinquency." *American Sociological Review* 45: 95–110.

Faith, Karlene, and Yasmin Jiwani. 2003. "The Social Construction of Dangerous Girls and Women." In Bernard Schissel and Carolyn Brooks.

Fedec, Kari. 2003. "Women and Children in Canada's Sex Trade: The Discriminatory Policing of the Marginalized." In Bernard Schissel and Carolyn Brooks.

Fleras, A., and J.L. Kunz. 2001. *Media and Minorities: Representing Diversity in a Multicultural Canada*. Toronto: Thompson Educational Publishing

Foucault, Michel. 1980. *Michel Foucault: Power and Knowledge*. London: Harvester Wheatsheaf.

Gartner, R., and A. Doob. 1994. "Trends in Criminal Victimization 1988–93." *Juristat Service Bulletin Canadian Center for Justice Statistics* 14 (13), Catalogue No. 85-002 XPB.

Gelsthorpe, Loraine, and Allison Morris. 1990. *Feminist Perspectives in Criminology*. Buckingham, UK: Open University Press.

Girard, Lina, and Steve Wormith. 2004. "The Predictive Validity of the Level of Service Inventory — Ontario Revision on General and Violent Recidivism among Various Offender Groups." *Criminal Justice and Behaviour* 31, 2: 150–81.

Giroux, Henry. 2000. Representations of Violence, Popular Culture and Demonization of Youth." In Stephanie Urso Spina (ed.), *Smoke and Mirrors: The Hidden Context of Violence in Schools and Society*. Lanham, MD: Rowman and Littlefield.

_____. 2003a. *The Abandoned Generation: Democracy Beyond the Culture of Fear*. New York: Palgrave MacMillan.

_____. 2003b. "Public Time and Educated Hope: Educational Leadership and the War Against Youth." *The Initiative Anthology*. Available at <www.muohio.edu/eduleadership/anthology/OA//OA03001.html) (accessed October 13, 2005).

Glassner, Barry. 1999. *The Culture of Fear: Why Americans Are Afraid of the Wrong Things*. New York: Basic Books.

Glor, Eleanor. 1989. "A Survey of Comprehensive Accident and Injury Experience of High School Students in Saskatchewan." *Canadian Journal of Public Health* 80: 435–40.

Goff, Colin, and Charles Reasons. 1978. *Corporate Crime in Canada*. Toronto: Prentice-Hall.

Goode, Erich, and Nachman Ben-Yehuda. 1994. *Moral Panics: The Social Construction of Deviance*. Oxford: Blackwell.

Green, Melvyn. 1986. "The History of Canadian Narcotics Control: The Formative Years." In Neil Boyd (ed.), *The Social Dimensions of Law*. Scarborough, ON: Prentice-Hall.

Green, R.G., and K. Healy. 2003. *Tough on Kids: Rethinking Approaches to Youth Justice*. Saskatoon, SK: Purich Publishing.

Griffith, C.T., and S. Verdon-Jones. 1994. *Canadian Criminal Justice* (Second ed.). Toronto: Harcourt Brace.

Grossberg, Lawrence. 2005. *Caught in the Crossfire: Kids, Politics and America's Future.* Boulder, CO: Paradigm.

Grossman, Dave. 1995. *On Killing: The Psychological Cost of Learning to Kill in War and Society.* Boston: Little Brown.

Hackett, Robert A. 1991. *News and Dissent: The Press and the Politics of Peace in Canada.* Norwood, NJ: Ablex Publishing.

Hale, C. 1989. "Economy, Punishment and Imprisonment." *Contemporary Crises* 13: 327–49.

Hall, Stuart, Chas Critcher, Tony Jefferson, John Clarke and Brian Roberts. 1978. *Policing the Crisis: Mugging, the State and Law and Order.* London: Macmillan.

Hamilton, A.C., and C.M. Sinclair. 1991. *Report of the Aboriginal Justice Inquiry of Manitoba. Volume 1: The System and Aboriginal People.* Winnipeg: Queen's Printer.

Healy, David. 2003. *Let Them Eat Prozac.* Toronto: Lorimer.

Hendricks, K.J., and L.A. Layne. 1999. "Adolescent Occupational Injuries in Fast Food Restaurants: An Examination of the Problem from a National Perspective." *Journal of Occupational and Environment Medicine* 41, 12: 1145–53.

Herman, Edward S., and Noam Chomsky. 1994. *Manufacturing Consent: The Political Economy of the Mass Media.* New York: Pantheon.

Hogeveen, B., and R.C. Smandych. 2001. "Origins of the Newly Proposed Canadian Youth Criminal Justice Act: Political Discourse and the Perceived Crisis in Youth Crime in the 1990s." In R.C. Smandych (ed.), *Youth Justice: History, Legislation, and Reform.* Toronto: Harcourt Canada.

Hollow Water. 1997. *The Four Circles of Hollowater: Ojibwa Circle, Offender Circle, Victim Circle, Hollow Water Circle.* Ottawa: Aboriginal Corretions Policy Unit.

Huculak, Judge Brian. 1995. "From the Power to Punish to the Power to Heal." *Justice as Healing: A Newsletter on Aboriginal Concepts of Justice.* Fall. Native Law Centre, University of Saskatchewan.

Hudson, Barbara. 2006. "Beyond White Man's Justice: Race, Gender, and Justice in Late Modernity." *Theoretical Criminology* 10, 1: 29–47.

Human Rights Watch (HRW). 2000. *Fingers to the Bone: United States Failure to Protect Child Farmworkers.* New York: Human Rights Watch.

Hunt, Alan. 1991. "Postmodernism and Critical Criminology." In Brian MacLean and Dragan Milovanovic (eds.), *New Directions in Critical Criminology.* Vancouver: Collective Press.

Hunter, Garson, and Dionne Miazdyck. 2006. "From Welfare to Workfare: Public Policy for the New Economy." In Dave Broad and Wayne Antony (eds.), *Capitalism Rebooted? Work, Welfare and the New Economy.* Halifax, NS: Fernwood.

Hylton, J.H. (1994). "Get Tough or Get Smart: Options for Canada's Youth Justice System in the Twenty-first Century." *Canadian Journal of Criminology,* 36: 229–46.

International Labour Organization (ILO). 2002. *A Future Without Child Labour.* Geneva.

_____. 2004. "Youth Employment at an All Time High." Press Release, August 11. Geneva.

Iyengar, Shanto, and Donald R. Kinder. 1987. *News That Matters.* Chicago: University of Chicago Press

Jenkins, Philip. 1992. *Intimate Enemies: Moral Panics in Contemporary Britain*. New York: Aldine de Gruyter.

Johnson, A.F. 1997. "Strengthening Society III: Social Security." In A.F. Johnson and A. Strich (eds.), *Canadian Public Policy: Globalization And Political Parties*. Toronto: Copp Clark.

Kaihla, Paul, John DeMont, and Chris Wood. 1994. "Kids Who Kill: Special Report." *Maclean's Magazine* August: 32–39.

Kappeler, Victor E., Mark Blumberg, and Gary W. Potter. 1993. *The Mythology of Crime and Delinquency*. Prospect Heights, Illinois: Waveland Press.

Kellner, Douglas. 1995. "Cultural Studies, Multiculturalism and Media Culture." In Gail Dines and Jean M. Humez (eds.), *Gender, Race and Class in Media: A Text Reader*. Thousand Oaks, CA: Sage.

Kelly, J. 1998. *Under the Gaze: Learning to be Black in White Society*. Halifax, NS: Fernwood.

Kershaw, A., and M. Lasovich. 1991. *Rock-A-Bye Baby: A Death Behind Bars*. Toronto: McClelland and Stewart.

Lafontaine, Tania, Sharon Acoose, and Bernard Schissel. 2005. *Healing Connections: Rising Above the Gangs*. Saskatoon, SK: White Buffalo Youth Lodge.

Landrigan, P., and R. Belville. 1993. "The Dangers of Illegal Child Labor." *American Journal of Diseases of Children* 147, 10: 1029–30.

Landrigan, Philip, and Jane McCammon. 1997. "Child Labour: Still With Us after all These Years." *Public Health Reports* 112: 466–73.

LaPrairie, Carol Pitcher. 1988. "The Young Offenders Act and Aboriginal Youth." In Joe Hudson, Joseph Hornick, and Barbara Burrows (eds.), *Justice and the Young Offender in Canada*. Toronto: Wall and Thompson.

LeBlanc, M. 1983. "Delinquency as an Epiphenomenon of Adolescence." In R. Corrado, M. Leblanc, and J. Trepanier (eds.), *Current Issues in Juvenile Justice*. Toronto: Butterworths.

Leishman, F., and P. Mason. 2003. *Policing and the Media: Facts, Fictions, and Factions*. Portland, OR: Willan Publishing.

Lowman, J. 1989. *Street Prostitution: Assessing the Impact of the Law (Vancouver)*. Ottawa: Minster of Justice and Attorney General of Canada, Department of Justice.

_____. 1991. "Understanding Prostitution in Canada: An Evaluation of the Brannigan-Fleischman Opportunity Model." *Canadian Journal of Law and Society* 6: 13–64.

Males, Mike. 1996. *Scapegoat Generation: America's War on Adolescents*. Monroe, ME: Common Courage.

_____. 2000. *Framing Youth: 10 Myths About the Next Generation*. Monroe, ME: Common Courage.

Massumi, Brian. 1993. *The Politics of Everyday Fear*. Minneapolis: University of Minnesota Press.

McBride, Steve. 2005. *Paradigm Shift: Globalization and the Canadian State* (Second edition). Halifax, NS: Fernwood Publishing.

McCormick, Chris. 1995. *Constructing Danger: The Mis/Representation of Crime in the News*. Halifax, NS: Fernwood Publishing.

McLuhan, Marshal. 1964. *Understanding Media: The Extensions of Man*. New York:

McGraw-Hill.

McMullan, John L. 2005. *News, Truth and Crime: The Westray Disaster and Its Aftermath.* Halifax, NS: Fernwood.

Miedzian, Miriam. 1998. *Boys will be Boys: Breaking the Links Between Masculinity and Violence.* Toronto: Doubleday.

Miller, Jerome. 1991. *Last One Over the Wall: The Massachusetts Experiment in Closing Reform Schools.* Coloumbus: Ohio State University Press.

Milner Jr., M. 2004. *Freaks, Geeks, and Cool Kids: American Teenagers, Schools, and the Culture of Consumption.* New York: Routledge.

Ministry of the Attorney General, Ontario. 2000. *2002–2003 Business Plan.* Toronto: Ministry of the Attorney General of Ontario.

Monture-Angus, Patricia. 1996. *Thunder in My Soul: A Mohawk Woman Speaks.* Halifax, NS: Fernwood Publishing.

Morris, Nomi. 1995. "Kids At Work." *Macleans* December 11: 28–29.

Morrison, B., P. Blood, and M. Thorsborne. 2005. "Practicing Restorative Justice in School Communities: Addressing the Challenge of Culture Change." *Public Organization Review* 5, 4: 335.

Newman, Tony. 2000. "Workers and Helpers: Perspectives on Children's Labour, 1899–1999. *British Journal of Social Work* 30: 323–38.

Nimmo, Melanie. 2001. *The "Invisible" Gang Members: A Report on Female Gang Association in Winnipeg.* Winnipeg, MB: Canadian Centre for Policy Alternatives.

Nyland, B. 1995. "Child Prostitution, and the New Australian Legislation on Paedophiles in Asia." *Journal of Contemporary Asia* 25, 4: 546–60.

O'Grady, Bill, and Carolyn Greene. 2003. "A Social and Economic Impact Study of the Ontario Safe Streets Act on Toronto Squeegee Workers." *Online Journal of Justice Studies* 1, 1. Available at <http://ojjs.icaap.org/issues/1.1/o'grady-greene.html> (accessed September 8, 2005).

O'Higgins, N. 2001. *Youth Unemployment and Employment Policy: A Global Perspective.* Geneva: International Labour Otganization.

O'Malley, Pat. 2000. "Risk Societies and the Government of Crime." In Mark Brown and John Pratt (eds.), *Dangerous Offenders: Punishment And Social Order.* New York: Routledge.

Painter, Kate. 1993. "The Mythology of Delinquency: An Empirical Critique." Presented at the British Criminology Conference, Cardiff University.

Parker, D.L. 1997. *Stolen Dreams: Portraits of Working Children.* Minneapolis: Lerner.

Philip, Margaret. 2003. "Middle-class FAS: A Silent Epidemic?" *Globe and Mail* February 1: F6.

Platt, Anthony. 1969. *The Child Savers: The Invention of Delinquency.* Chicago: University of Chicago Press.

Popenoe, David. 1998. "Life Without Father." In Cynthia Daniels.

Postman, Neil. 1985. *Amusing Ourselves to Death: Public Discourse in the Age of Show Business.* New York: Penguin.

_____. 1988. *Conscientious Objections: Stirring Up Trouble About Language, Technology, and Education.* New York: Alfred A. Knopf.

_____. 1994. *The Disappearance of Childhood.* New York: Vintage.

Poulantzas, Nicos. 1972. "The Problem of the Capitalist State." In Robin Blackburn (ed.), *Ideology in the Social Sciences*. New York: Pantheon Books.

Pratt, John. 2000. "Dangerousness and Modern Society." In Mark Brown and John Pratt (eds.), *Dangerous Offenders: Punishment and Social Order*. New York: Routledge.

Quewezance, Helen, and Wendy Schissel. 2003. "Damaged Children and Broken Spirits: A Residential School Survivor's Story." In B. Schissel and C. Brooks.

Quinney, Richard. 1974. *Critique of Legal Order: Crime Control in Capitalist Society*. Boston: Little, Brown.

Ramazanoglu, Caroline. 1993. *Up Against Foucault: Explorations of Some Tensions Between Foucault and Feminism*. London: Routledge.

Reid-MacNevin, Susan. 1991. "A Theoretical Understanding of Current Canadian Juvenile-Justice Policy." In Alan Leschied, Peter Jaffe, and Wayne Willis (eds.), *The Young Offenders Act: A Revolution in Canadian Juvenile Justice*. Toronto: University of Toronto Press.

Reiter, Ester. 1996. *Making Fast Food: From the Frying Pan into the Fryer*. Montreal: McGill University Press.

Robbins, R.H. 2005. *Global Problems and the Culture of Capitalism* (Third ed.). Boston: Allyn and Bacon

Roberts, D., and U.G. Foehr. 2004. *Kids and the Media in America*. Cambridge, MA: Cambridge University Press.

Robinson, Laura. 1998. *Crossing the Line: Violence and Sexual Assault in Canada's National Sport*. Toronto: McLelland and Stewart.

Rosenau, Pauline M. 1992. *Postmodernism and the Social Sciences: Insights, Inroads, and Intrusions*. Princeton, NJ: Princeton University Press.

Ross, Rupert. 1993. *Dancing with a Ghost: Exploring Indian Reality*. Markham, ON: Octopus Publishing.

_____. 1995. "Aboriginal Community Healing in Action: The Hollow Water Approach." *Justice as Healing: A Newsletter on Aboriginal Concepts of Justice*. Native Law Centre, University of Saskatchewan.

Ryan, Joan. 1995. *Doing Things the Right Way: Dene Traditional Justice in Lac La Marte, N.W.T.* Calgary: University of Calgary Press.

Ryan, William. 1976. *Blaming the Victim*. New York: Vintage.

Sachs, A. 1994. "The Last Commodity: Child Prostitution in the Developing World." *World Watch* July/August: 24–30.

Saskatchewan Justice. 2004. *Saskatchewan Commission on First Nations and Metis People and Justice Reform*. Regina: Government of Saskatchewan.

Schiraldi, Vincent, and Jason Zeidenberg. 1997. *The Risks Juveniles Face When They are Incarcerated with Adults*. San Francisco: Center on Juvenile and Criminal Justice.

Schissel, Bernard. 1992. "The Influence of Economic Factors and Social Control Policy on Crime Rate Changes in Canada (1962–1988)." *Canadian Journal of Sociology* 17, 4: 405–28.

_____. 1993. *The Social Dimensions of Canadian Youth Justice*. Don Mills, ON: Oxford University Press.

_____. 1995a. "Trends in Official Crime Rates." In James Creechan and Robert

Silverman (eds.), *Canadian Delinquency*. Scarborough, ON: Prentice-Hall.

_____. 1995b. "Degradation, Social Deprivation and Violence: Health Risks for Women Prisoners." In B. Singh Bolaria and Rosemary Bolaria (eds.), *Women, Minorities and Health*. Toronto: Fernwood Publishing.

_____. 1997. *Blaming Children: Youth Crime, Moral Panics, and the Politics of Hate*. Halifax, NS: Fernwood Publishing.

_____. 2003. "Youth Crime, Youth Justice, and the Politics of Marginalization." In Bernard Schissel and Carolyn Brooks.

Schissel, Bernard, and Carolyn Brooks (eds.). 2003. *Marginality and Condemnation: An Introduction to Critical Criminology*. Halifax, NS: Fernwood Publishing.

Schissel, Bernard, and Terry Wotherspoon. 2003. *The Legacy of School for Aboriginal People: Education, Oppression, and Emancipation*. Toronto: Oxford University Press.

Schlosser, Eric. 2002. *Fast Food Nation: The Dark Side of the All-American Meal*. Boston: Houghton Mifflin.

Shaver, Fran. "Prostitution: A Female Crime?" In E. Adelberg and C. Currie (eds.), *In Conflict with the Law: Women and the Canadian Justice System*. Vancouver: Press Gang.

Shaw, Margaret. 2000. "Women, Violence and Disorders in Prison." In Kelly Hannah-Moffat and Margaret Shaw (eds.), *An Ideal Prison? Critical Essays on Women's Imprisonment in Canada*. Halifax, NS: Fernwood Publishing.

Shragge, Eric. 1997. *Workfare: Ideology for a New Underclass*. Toronto: Garamond.

Smart, Carol. 1990. "Feminist Approaches to Criminology or Postmodern Women Meets Atavsitic Man." In Loraine Gelsthorpe and Allison Morris (eds.), *Feminist Perspectives in Criminology*. Buckingham, UK: Open University Press.

Snyder, Howard N., and Melissa Sickmund. 1995. *Juvenile Offenders and Victims: A National Report*. Washington, DC: Office of Juvenile Justice and Delinquency Prevention.

Southern Ontario Newspaper Guild. 2005. *Journalistic Standards in Monopolized Media*. Available at <www.song.on.ca/journalist_standards.html> (accessed October 5, 2005).

_____. N.D. Available at <www.song.on.ca/journalist_standards> (accessed June 2006).

Stroud, Carsten. 1993. *Contempt of Court: the Betrayal of Justice in Canada?* Toronto: MacMillan.

Stuart, Judge Barry. 1993. "Community-Based Justice Initiatives: An Overview." *Seeking Common Ground*, publication from the 21st International Conference, Society of Professionals in Dispute Resolution (SPIDR). Toronto, October.

Sutherland, Anne, and Beth Thompson. 2003. *Kidfluence: The Marketers Guide to Understanding and Reaching Generation Y: Kids, Tweens, and Teens*. New York: McGraw-Hill.

Tanner, Julian. 1996. *Teenage Troubles: Youth And Deviance In Canada*. Toronto: Nelson Canada.

Teeple. Gary. 2000. *Globalization and the Decline of Social Welfare into the 21st Century*. Aurora, ON: Garamond.

Tustin, Lee, and Robert Lutes. 2006. *A Guide to the Youth Criminal Justice Act*. Markham,

ON: LexisNexis Butterworths.

Underdown, David. 1992. *Fire From Heaven: Life in an English Town in the Seventeenth Century*. London: Harper Collins.

United States Department of Labour. 2002. "Lost Worktime Injuries and Illnesses: Characteristics and Resulting Days Away from Work, 2001." In *NEWS* Washington: Bureau of Labor Statistics.

Usalcas, Jeannine. 2005. "Youth and the Labour Market." *Perspectives*, Statistics Canada, Catalogue No. 75-001-XIE.

Wachtel, T. 2003. "Restorative Justice in Everyday Life: Beyond the Formal Ritual." *Reclaiming Children & Youth* 12, 2: 83.

Watts, Richard. 2004. "The Frightening Irony of Fetal Alcohol Syndrome." *Times Colonist* March 9: D1.

West, Gordon. 1991. "Towards a More Socially Informed Understanding of Canadian Delinquency Legislation." In Alan Leschied, Peter Jaffe, and Wayne Willis (eds.), *The Young Offenders Act: A Revolution in Canadian Juvenile Justice*. Toronto: University of Toronto Press.

White, Jeff. 2001. "When it Comes to Alcohol, It's Time to Start Discriminating Against Aboriginals." *The Report Magazine* April 16: 1.

Winterdyk, John A. 1996. "Trends and Patterns in Youth Crime." In John Winterdyk (ed.), *Issues and Perspectives on Young Offenders In Canada*, Toronto: Harcourt Brace.

_____. 2000. *Issues and Perspectives on Young Offenders In Canada*. Toronto: Thomson/ Nelson.

York, Geoffrey. 1990. *The Dispossessed: Life and Death in Native Canada*. Toronto: Little Brown and Company.

Young, Alison. 1996. *Imagining Crime: Textual Outlaws and Criminal Conversations*. London: Sage.